"Captures today's scooter scene"

SCOOTER
Lifestyle

VELOCE

Ian 'Iggy' Grainger

SpeedPro Series
4-Cylinder Engine – How to Blueprint & Build a Short Block for High Performance (Hammill)
Alfa Romeo DOHC High-Performance Manual)Kartalamakis)
Alfa Romeo V6 Engine High-Performance Manual (Kartalamakis)
BMC 998cc A-Series Engine – How to Power Tune (Hammill)
1275cc A-Series High-Performance Manual (Hammill)
Camshafts – How to Choose & Time them for Maximum Power (Hammill)
Cylinder Heads – How to Build, Modify & Power Tune Updated & Revised Edition (Burgess & Gollan)
Distributor-type Ignition Systems – How to Build & Power Tune (Hammill)
Fast Road Car – How to Plan and Build Revised & Updated Colour New Edition (Stapleton)
Ford SOHC 'Pinto' & Sierra Cosworth DOHC Engines – How to Power Tune Updated & Enlarged Edition (Hammill)
Ford V8 – How to Power Tune Small Block Engines (Hammill)
Harley-Davidson Evolution Engines – How to Build & Power Tune (Hammill)
Holley Carburetors – How to Build & Power Tune Revised & Updated Edition (Hammill)
Jaguar XK Engines – How to Power Tune Revised & Updated Colour Edition (Hammill)
MG Midget & Austin-Healey Sprite – How to Power Tune Updated & Revised Edition (Stapleton)
MGB 4-Cylinder Engine – How to Power Tune (Burgess)
MGB V8 Power – How to Give Your, Third Colour Edition (Williams)
MGB, MGC & MGB V8 – How to Improve (Williams)
Mini Engines – How to Power Tune on a Small Budget Colour Edition (Hammill)
Motorcycle-engined Racing Car – How to Build (Pashley)
Motorsport – Getting Started (Collins)
Motorsports Datalogging (Templeman)
Nitrous Oxide High-Performance Manual (Langfield)
Rover V8 Engines – How to Power Tune (Hammill)
Sportscar/Kitcar Suspension & Brakes – How to Build & Modify Enlarged & Updated 2nd Edition (Hammill)
SU Carburettor High-Performance Manual (Hammill)
Supercar, How to Build (Thompson)
Suzuki 4x4 – How to Modify for Serious Off-Road Action (Richardson)
Tiger Avon Sportscar – How to Build Your Own Updated & Revised 2nd Edition (Dudley)
TR2, 3 & TR4 – How to Improve (Williams)
TR5, 250 & TR6 – How to Improve (Williams)
TR7 & TR8, How to Improve (Williams)
V8 Engine – How to Build a Short Block for High Performance (Hammill)
Volkswagen Beetle Suspension, Brakes & Chassis – How to Modify for High Performance (Hale)
Volkswagen Bus Suspension, Brakes & Chassis – How to Modify for High Performance (Hale)
Weber DCOE, & Dellorto DHLA Carburetors – How to Build & Power Tune 3rd Edition (Hammill)

Those were the days ... Series
Alpine Trials & Rallies 1910-1973 (Pfundner)
Austerity Motoring (Bobbitt)
Brighton National Speed Trials (Gardiner)
British Police Cars (Walker)
British Woodies (Peck)
Crystal Palace by (Collins)
Dune Buggy Phenomenon (Hale)
Dune Buggy Phenomenon Volume 2 (Hale)
Hot Rod & Stock Car Racing in Britain in the 1980s (Neil)
MG's Abingdon Factory (Moylan)
Motor Racing at Brands Hatch in the Seventies (Parker)
Motor Racing at Goodwood in the Sixties (Gardiner)
Motor Racing at Oulton Park in the 1960s (McFadyen)
Motor Racing at Oulton Park in the 1970s (McFadyen)
Three Wheelers (Bobbitt)

Enthusiast's Restoration Manual Series
Citroën 2CV, How to Restore (Porter)
Classic Car Bodywork, How to Restore (Thaddeus)
Classic Car Electrics (Thaddeus)
Classic Cars, How to Paint (Thaddeus)
Reliant Regal, How to Restore (Payne)
Triumph TR2/3/3A, How to Restore (Williams)
Triumph TR4/4A, How to Restore (Williams)
Triumph TR5/250 & 6, How to Restore (Williams)
Triumph TR7/8, How to Restore (Williams)
Volkswagen Beetle, How to Restore (Tyler)
VW Bay Window Bus (Paxton)
Yamaha FS1-E, How to Restore (Watts)

Essential Buyer's Guide Series
Alfa GT (Booker)
Alfa Romeo Spider Giulia (Booker & Talbott)
BMW GS (Henshaw)
BSA Bantam (Henshaw)
BSA Twins (Henshaw)
Citroën 2CV (Paxton)
Citroën ID & DS (Heilig)
Fiat 500 & 600 (Bobbitt)
Jaguar E-type 3.8 & 4.2-litre (Crespin)
Jaguar E-type V12 5.3-litre (Crespin)
Jaguar/Daimler XJ6, XJ12 & Sovereign (Crespin)
Jaguar XJ-S (Crespin)
MGB & MGB GT (Williams)
Mercedes-Benz 280SL-560SL Roadsters (Bass)
Mercedes-Benz 'Pagoda' 230SL, 250SL & 280SL Roadsters & Coupés (Bass)
Morris Minor (Newell)
Porsche 928 (Hemmings)

Rolls-Royce Silver Shadow & Bentley T-Series (Bobbitt)
Subaru Impreza (Hobbs)
Triumph Bonneville (Henshaw)
Triumph TR6 (Williams)
VW Beetle (Cservenka & Copping)
VW Bus (Cservenka & Copping)

Auto-Graphics Series
Fiat-based Abarths (Sparrow)
Jaguar MkI & II Saloons (Sparrow)
Lambretta LI series scooters (Sparrow)

Rally Giants Series
Audi Quattro (Robson)
Big Healey – 100-Six & 3000 (Robson)
Ford Escort MkI (Robson)
Ford Escort RS1800 (Robson)
Lancia Stratos (Robson)
Peugeot 205 T16 (Robson)
Subaru Impreza (Robson)

General
1¹/₂-litre GP Racing 1961-1965 (Whitelock)
AC Two-litre Saloons & Buckland Sportscars (Archibald)
According to Carter (Skelton)
Alfa Romeo Giulia Coupé GT & GTA (Tipler)
Alfa Romeo Montreal - The Essential Companion (Taylor)
Alfa Tipo 33 (McDonough & Collins)
Anatomy of the Works Minis (Moylan)
Armstrong-Siddeley (Smith)
Autodrome (Collins & Ireland)
Automotive A-Z, Lane's Dictionary of Automotive Terms (Lane)
Automotive Mascots (Kay & Springate)
Bahamas Speed Weeks, The (O'Neil)
Bentley Continental, Corniche and Azure (Bennett)
Bentley MkVI, Rolls-Royce Silver Wraith, Dawn & Cloud/Bentley R & S-series (Nutland)
BMC Competitions Department Secrets (Turner, Chambers Browning)
BMW 5-Series (Cranswick)
BMW Z-Cars (Taylor)
British 250cc Racing Motorcycles by Chris Pereira
British Cars, The Complete Catalogue of, 1895-1975 (Culshaw & Horrobin)
BRM – a mechanic's tale (Salmon)
BRM V16 (Ludvigsen)
BSA Bantam Bible (Henshaw)
Bugatti Type 40 (Price)
Bugatti 46/50 Updated Edition (Price & Arbey)
Bugatti T44 & T49 (Price & Arbey)
Bugatti 57 2nd Edition (Price)
Caravans, The Illustrated History 1919-1959 (Jenkinson)
Caravans, The Illustrated History from 1960 (Jenkinson)
Carrera Panamericana (Tipler)
Chrysler 300 – America's Most Powerful Car 2nd Edition (Ackerson)
Chrysler PT Cruiser (Ackerson)
Citroën DS (Bobbitt)
Cliff Alison - From the Fells to Ferrari (Gauld)
Cobra – The Real Thing! (Legate)
Cortina – Ford's Bestseller (Robson)
Coventry Climax Racing Engines (Hammill)
Daimler SP250 New Edition (Long)
Datsun Fairlady Roadster to 280ZX – The Z-car Story (Long)
Dino – The V6 Ferrari (Long)
Dodge Charger – Enduring Thunder (Ackerson)
Dodge Dynamite! (Grist)
Draw & Paint Cars – How to (Gardiner)
Drive on the Wild Side, A – 20 extreme driving adventures from around the world (Weaver)
Ducati 750 Bible, The (Falloon)
Ducati 860, 900 and Mille Bible, The (Falloon)
Dune Buggy, Building a – The Essential Manual (Shakespeare)
Dune Buggy Files (Hale)
Dune Buggy Handbook (Hale)
Edward Turner: the man behind the motorcycles (Clew)
Fiat & Abarth 124 Spider & Coupé (Tipler)
Fiat & Abarth 500 & 600 2nd edition (Bobbitt)
Fiats, Great Small (Ward)
Fine Art of the Motorcycle Engine, The (Peirce)
Ford F100/F150 Pick-up 1948-1996 (Ackerson)
Ford F150 1997-2005 (Ackerson)
Ford GT – Then, and Now (Streather)
Ford GT40 (Legate)
Ford in Miniature (Olson)
Ford Model Y (Roberts)
Ford Thunderbird from 1954, The Book of the (Long)
Forza Minardi! (Vigar)
Funky Mopeds (Skelton)
Gentleman Jack (Gauld)
GM in Miniature (Olson)
GT – The World's Best GT Cars 1953-73 (Dawson)
Hillclimbing & Sprinting – The essential manual (Short & Wilkinson)
Honda NSX (Long)
Jaguar, The Rise of (Price)
Jaguar XJ-S (Long)
Jeep CJ (Ackerson)
Jeep Wrangler (Ackerson)
Karmann-Ghia Coupé & Convertible (Bobbitt)
Lambretta Bible, The (Davies)
Lancia 037 (Collins)
Lancia Delta HF Integrale (Blaettel & Wagner)
Land Rover, The Half-Ton Military (Cook)
Laverda Twins & Triples Bible 1968-1986 (Falloon)

Lea-Francis Story, The (Price)
Lexus Story, The (Long)
little book of smart, the (Jackson)
Lola – The Illustrated History (1957-1977) (Starkey)
Lola – All the Sports Racing & Single-Seater Racing Cars 1978-1997 (Starkey)
Lola T70 – The Racing History & Individual Chassis Record 4th Edition (Starkey)
Lotus 49 (Oliver)
MarketingMobiles, The Wonderful Wacky World of (Hale)
Mazda MX-5/Miata 1.6 Enthusiast's Workshop Manual (Grainger & Shoemark)
Mazda MX-5/Miata 1.8 Enthusiast's Workshop Manual (Grainger & Shoemark)
Mazda MX-5 Miata: the book of the world's favourite sportscar (Long)
Mazda MX-5 Miata Roadster (Long)
MGA (Price Williams)
MGB & MGB GT – Expert Guide (Auto-Doc Series) (Williams)
MGB Electrical Systems (Astley)
Micro Caravans (Jenkinson)
Micro Trucks (Mort)
Microcars at large! (Quellin)
Mini Cooper – The Real Thing! (Tipler)
Mitsubishi Lancer Evo, the road car & WRC story (Long)
Montlhéry, the story of the Paris autodrome (Boddy)
Morgan Maverick (Lawrence)
Morris Minor, 60 years on the road (Newell)
Moto Guzzi Sport & Le Mans Bible (Falloon)
Motor Movies – The Posters! (Veysey)
Motor Racing – Reflections of a Lost Era (Carter)
Motorcycle Road & Racing Chassis Designs (Noakes)
Motorhomes, The Illustrated History (Jenkinson)
Motorsport in colour, 1950s (Wainwright)
Nissan 300ZX & 350Z – The Z-Car Story (Long)
Pass the Theory and Practical Driving Tests (Gibson & Hoole)
Peking to Paris 2007 (Young)
Plastic Toy Cars of the 1950s & 1960s (Ralston)
Pontiac Firebird (Cranswick)
Porsche Boxster (Long)
Porsche 356 (2nd edition) (Long)
Porsche 911 Carrera – The Last of the Evolution (Corlett)
Porsche 911R, RS & RSR, 4th Edition (Starkey)
Porsche 911 – The Definitive History 1963-1971 (Long)
Porsche 911 – The Definitive History 1971-1977 (Long)
Porsche 911 – The Definitive History 1977-1987 (Long)
Porsche 911 – The Definitive History 1987-1997 (Long)
Porsche 911 – The Definitive History 1997-2004 (Long)
Porsche 911SC 'Super Carrera' – The Essential Companion (Streather)
Porsche 914 & 914-6: The Definitive History Of The Road & Competition Cars (Long)
Porsche 924 (Long)
Porsche 944 (Long)
Porsche 993 'King of Porsche' – The Essential Companion (Streather)
Porsche 996 'Supreme Porsche' – The Essential Companion (Streather)
Porsche Racing Cars – 1953 to 1975 (Long)
Porsche Racing Cars – 1976 on (Long)
Porsche – The Rally Story (Meredith)
Porsche: Three Generations of Genius (Meredith)
RAC Rally Action! (Gardiner)
Rallye Sport Fords: the inside story (Moreton)
Redman, Jim – 6 Times World Motorcycle Champion: The Autobiography (Redman)
Rolls-Royce Silver Shadow/Bentley T Series Corniche & Camargue Revised & Enlarged Edition (Bobbitt)
Rolls-Royce Silver Spirit, Silver Spur & Bentley Mulsanne 2nd Edition (Bobbitt)
RX-7 – Mazda's Rotary Engine Sportscar (updated & revised new edition) (Long)
Scooters & Microcars, The A-Z of popular (Dan)
Scooter Lifestyle (Grainger)
Singer Story: Cars, Commercial Vehicles, Bicycles & Motorcycles (Atkinson)
SM – Citroën's Maserati-engined Supercar (Long & Claverol)
Subaru Impreza: the road car and WRC story (Long)
Taxi! The Story of the 'London' Taxicab (Bobbitt)
Tinplate Toy Cars of the 1950s & 1960s (Ralston)
Toyota Celica & Supra, the book of Toyota's Sports Coupés (Long)
Toyota MR2 Coupés & Spyders (Long)
Triumph Motorcycles & the Meriden Factory (Hancox)
Triumph Speed Twin & Thunderbird Bible (Woolridge)
Triumph Tiger Cub Bible (Estall)
Triumph Trophy Bible (Woolridge)
Triumph TR6 (Kimberley)
Unraced (Collins)
Velocette Motorcycles – MSS to Thruxton Updated & Revised (Burris)
Virgil Exner – Visioneer: The official biography of Virgil M Exner designer extraordinaire (Grist)
Volkswagen Bus Book, The (Bobbitt)
Volkswagen Bus or Van to Camper, How to Convert (Porter)
Volkswagens of the World (Glen)
VW Beetle Cabriolet (Bobbitt)
VW Beetle – The Car of the 20th Century (Copping)
VW Bus – 40 years of Splitties, Bays & Wedges (Copping)
VW Bus Book, The (Bobbitt)
VW Golf: five generations of fun (Copping & Cservenka)
VW – The air-cooled era (Copping)
VW T5 Camper Conversion Manual (Porter)
VW Campers (Copping)
Works Minis, The Last (Purves & Brenchley)
Works Rally Mechanic (Moylan)

First published in April 2008 by Veloce Publishing Limited, 33 Trinity Street, Dorchester DT1 1TT, England. Fax 01305 268864/e-mail info@veloce.co.uk/web www.veloce.co.uk or www.velocebooks.com.
ISBN: 978-1-845841-52-2/UPC: 6-36847-04152-6
Readers with ideas for automotive books, or books on other transport or related hobby subjects, are invited to write to the editorial director of Veloce Publishing at the above address.
British Library Cataloguing in Publication Data - A catalogue record for this book is available from the British Library. Typesetting, design and page make-up all by Veloce Publishing Ltd on Apple Mac.
Printed in India by Replika Press.

Contents

Foreword, Dedication & Thanks

Foreword

To be able to produce a book on any subject the writer has to have a full command of the subject concerned. Iggy is a long-time dedicated Scooterist, and has exceptional knowledge of the history of scootering. In this book he offers you a view of scootering that will stand good for many years. The 'visual' way in which Iggy has portrayed scooters will, I'm sure, give the reader a great deal of pleasure.

It's a delight for me to pen the foreword on this book, for what I believe to be a picture window on scootering, which has come a long way from those heady days of the '50s when the demand for cheap transport after the war spawned a plethora of scooters.

Thanks to the twin pillars of scooter manufacture, Innocenti and Piaggio, scootering has evolved into a huge pastime for many thousands of people. It is without doubt a great hobby.

It is understandable that such a popular pastime should give birth to other facets within itself, i.e. music, customising, restoration, sport, etc. Add to that the social climate which rotates around the runs, custom shows, parts fairs, weekenders, and lots of other gatherings. The saying that scootering is a 'way of life' says it all.

From the Mods in the '60s right up to today, being a Scooterist is a way of life. I've enjoyed a fantastic time being a Scooterist, and have always been proud to be one; from my early days in Glasgow, using a scooter to get to work, and years later, becoming national road race champion, Vespa club champion, and UK sprint champion.

This book depicts scootering with all the nuts and bolts, chrome, restoration, customising, and the sporting side. Comprehensive and informative, leaf through the pages and enjoy the view, there's none better.

Norrie Kerr

Dedication

This book is dedicated to all the scooter riders who regularly ride their ill-powered shopping bikes the length and breadth of the British Isles in search of a good time. If it's worth going, it's worth going on your scooter!

Thanks

Thanks to the following people for help, encouragement and additional archive photos for this book: Norrie Kerr (a true gent), Steve Foster, Dave Porter, Jay C, Gray Gee, Bry Gee, Paula T, Chris Hamilton, Matty, Dave Gould, Andy Gillard, Mau Spencer, Morton's Motorcycle Media, Jeff Johnson, Nik Skeat and Terry Walters. Thanks also to Rod Grainger at Veloce for taking the project on, and to, Kate Clifford and Gary Jones for their help. Thanks also to Graham Fisher for posing for the cover shot

Special thanks to Linsey, Millie, Ella and my parents for finally leaving me alone to finish it on time, after weeks of subtle hints!

Publisher's note

The older photographs in this book are poor quality snapshots, but are important to the story.

Introduction

There's been plenty said and written about scooters over the years, but until now there's been no definitive look at the culture surrounding our chosen way of life. Many authors have written about Mods or the infamous and often over-hyped beach battles of the 1960s, but few have tried to capture the atmosphere of the modern scene.

I wanted to share some of my early experiences and take a look at the scene from the inside. I've not mentioned music too much, because it's far too diverse these days to do it any justice, and the book would have had to have been an A-Z to fit in all the popular genres of music you'll hear at rallies and events!

Instead, I've concentrated on a nostalgic trip through time; from my early discovery of this all consuming hobby, to the present scene. You'll find scooter rallies and racing, customs, alliances and the history of the last quarter of a century since I was introduced to this way of life. Yes, it sounds like a long time when you say it like that doesn't it?

You'll notice that Mods aren't too well covered in this book, that's because they've occupied more than enough column inches over the years, and there are plenty of books available which look exclusively at their world.

We still owe the original Mods for fuelling the imagination of past, present and future generations of scooter riders, for leaving a legacy of rich scooter history behind them, and without them we probably wouldn't be here enjoying the scene.

Although the Mod way of life was the spark which lit the fuse for many of us, the majority of scooter riders have evolved into lifestyle Scooterists. We may not dress in a particular style and our scooters may not be adorned with lights and mirrors but we still burn with the same passion as our scooter riding ancestors.

It's over sixty years since the first scooters rolled off the Italian production lines, but there is still a buzzing and vibrant lifestyle with the humble scooter as its nucleus. The small capacity machines have overtaken the lives of thousands of us, often to the detriment of everything else we hold dear. Careers, relationships and families have suffered for this overwhelming and expensive addiction. An addiction to which there is no cure. We live and breathe the sickly sweet smell of synthetic two-stroke oil, and worship at the altar of our chosen gods, Lambretta and Vespa (or occasionally Gilera and Italjet). Our hands are permanently ingrained with the oily 'tattoos' of a thousand engine rebuilds, and our major organs have suffered the long term effects of our hedonistic binge drinking, hard partying, sleepless, junk food eating, nomadic lifestyle.

This book will take you on a journey of discovery, a road trip across the modern road going scooter scene in all its diversities. The ride may not always be a smooth one, and there's every chance you'll suffer mishaps along the way, but persevere because there's a town full of your closest friends at the end of the journey. You'll arrive tired, dishevelled and possibly strapped onto the back of a recovery truck, but it'll be worth it in the end ... Enjoy the ride.

1

The wonder years

I'd grown up, a child of the seventies, with three heroes. My first was a lad called Kevin who lived in a council house three doors down from us in Ilkeston, Derbyshire. Kevin was at least ten years older than me and he owned a big, noisy, green Kawasaki Z1, and I quickly grew to love all things with two wheels. My other heroes were Barry Sheene and the world's favourite stunt rider, Evel Knievel. I had the stunt set with wind-up Evel Knievel motorbike, which would wheelie across the carpet and crash spectacularly into the skirting board, or jump over carefully-constructed ramps made from a *Blue Peter* annual and Lego blocks. Regrettably, I fastened Evel into my Action Man's parachute harness one day and my plastic stunt rider accidentally crash-landed into my Grandma's guttering, where he remained for the next fifteen years. His star-spangled suit was ruined by the time the mouldy daredevil was eventually rescued by the council workmen who modernised the house many years later. It was a leap too far for Evel.

It was a forgone conclusion that I'd end up involved with bikes or scooters at some stage in the future. By the time I was eight we'd moved to Nottinghamshire and I'd worn down my parents with my constant pleas for a motorbike. Christmas arrived and I opened my presents, which included an open-faced helmet and a red motorbike suit. I was thrilled, but still wanted the bike to go with them;

sadly, my parents said they couldn't afford the bike ... Mum asked me to make her a cup of tea and, when I walked into the kitchen, there it was, gleaming in all its Italian redness.

I'd like to say that what stood in the kitchen was a brand new Lambretta, but at the time I'd

My first bike. The gears and my impatient tutor put me off, so it was, regrettably, sold!

school started wearing parkas with Mod patches and Union Jacks sewn onto them. Being young and impressionable I was drawn to this new fashion and I raided the stash of old sixties records in our loft, finding a few Who LPs, the odd Small Faces single, and a couple of Kinks records. I was gutted when a friend discovered The Who record *My Generation* in his dad's collection, the 1965 record was worth a fortune at the time.

Before long we had a gang of around 35 young Mods in our secondary school; not bad for a Nottinghamshire pit village. Being a Mod helped to build bridges between kids who were otherwise divided by the Miners' Strike, opposing sides in a fight we didn't really understand, but one that our dads either believed in or were bitterly opposed to. Times were tough in the early eighties.

We lived, ate and breathed scooters, even though we were all still too young to ride one, and many of us had never even sat on one. Naturally, we formed our own scooter club, the Notts Warriors SC, and eventually had around 40 members from school. As word spread, Mods from other local towns and villages joined as well. Hardly anyone in the club was old enough to ride a scooter in the early days, or even buy a pint of beer, but we saved our 50p a week subs and had club back-patches printed by Paddy Smith (with a scooter-riding, beer-swilling cartoon of Hagar the Horrible), and knew that one day we'd be sixteen and able to hit the roads at last.

In May 1985 one of the lads arrived at school with a new magazine devoted to our chosen way of life. Issue one of *Scootering Magazine* had arrived in the newsagents and our young minds were filled with images of custom

have been disappointed if it had been. I was thrilled to bits with my Tecnomoto 50, it may have been a motorbike but at least it was Italian, and just like a scooter it took some starting! The trials bike was fantastic; it had a six-speed gearbox and did sixty miles per hour. Unfortunately, I was crap at riding it; I just couldn't master changing gear. My planned appearance on *Junior Kickstart* lay in tatters, and my dad's patience was wearing thin, so before the following year was over the bike had been sold. My love for two wheels remained, though, but lay dormant for the next few years.

I started noticing scooters for the first time as we made our frequent trips to Chapel St. Leonards for weekends in our caravan. Passing the boring hours in the back of the car I'd notice groups of strange-looking scooters with what seemed like tons of luggage strapped to the back. The scooters always wobbled and got blown about by the wind, but it looked like a much better option than going away for the weekend in a car. It was a couple more years before I realised where these scooter riders were heading for the weekend, and why.

My own introduction to this exciting 'new' world started in 1983. A few older lads at

SCOOTER LIFESTYLE

scooters, rallies, and pictures of exciting-looking scooter parts and accessories. Not much work got done at school that day!

I ordered the magazine from Joe Squires, the local newsagent, and waited for what seemed like years to get my own copy. Finally it arrived and I read the magazine from cover to cover. That was almost a quarter of a century ago and I've read every issue since and still keep them safely tucked away in boxes in the overloaded attic at my parents' house.

One advert in the new magazine which caught our young eyes (like rabbits caught in a Lambretta's 6-volt headlight) was for a scooter rally just a few miles down the road from where we lived. DISC '85, or 'Donington International Scooter Classic' to give it its full name, was sponsored by Vespa UK, and it featured top scooter style bands of the time, like Bad Manners and The Meteors, as well as scooter racing, a massive custom show and, more importantly, wet t-shirt competitions. One way or another, we had to be there. As well as never having sat on a scooter, most of us had never seen a naked breast either – so Donington looked like it'd open our young eyes in more ways than one.

As luck would have it a mate's dad drove coaches for a living and we bullied him into hiring one for us. The list went around school, deposits were taken and, within days, the 53-seater, single-decker was full to capacity. Unfortunately for us the driver was working on the Saturday, so we could only go for Sunday. Little did we know that all the action happens on Friday and Saturday night and most people would be packing up to go home by the time we arrived!

As the rally slowly approached I spent many long nights poring over my only copy of *Scootering Magazine* to see what kind of clothes people wore to rallies (in a desperate attempt to fit in). At the time I was a

self-respecting young Mod, and usually wore desert boots and jeans with a button-down shirt and inch wide tie – don't laugh, it's all I could afford from my pocket money! I even remember creosoting the garden fence one Saturday whilst wearing my best Mod gear; naturally, I ended up with brown stains on my favourite (and only) shirt!

Looking at the photos of rallies and events in *Scootering* it seemed like the times were changing and

the new breed of scooter rider had cast aside Mod attire in favour of a more practical alternative. Combat trousers, printed t-shirts and Doc Martins or Rockabilly-style 'winkle pickers' seemed to be the order of the day, so I persuaded my mum to buy me some. She wouldn't get me any scruffy old Army surplus combats, though, so I had to make do with a pair of smart black fashion ones instead, with zips down the legs, and a pair of cheap suede winkle pickers from Jonathon James, worn with the obligatory white socks, of course. I also got a cheap, green MA1 flight jacket from Yeomans Army Stores to complete my new image. It wasn't the Alpha jacket I really wanted but it would have to do.

After an agonising wait, the all important weekend finally arrived. On Saturday morning I spent the day shopping in Nottingham with my grandma and bought the new Style Council LP, *Walls Come Tumbling Down*, in Victoria Centre market (all good Scooter Boys shop with granny!) I remember the hairs on the back of my neck standing on end as I heard a news bulletin reporting that ten thousand Mods had "invaded Donington Park". The next day we'd be a part of it.

A sleepless night later and we set off on the journey of a lifetime to Donington for the rally. The coach was full of boisterous spotty-faced juveniles, wearing a strange combination of parkas, boating blazers, flight jackets and denims. We got overly excited at every scooter we saw on the half-hour journey south along the M1. We didn't seem to notice that they were all travelling the other way, though!

As we scrambled off the coach and parted with our fiver to get in, the sight that greeted us was unbelievable, despite many people having already left the race circuit there were still thousands of scooters, Mods, and Scooter Boys everywhere, as far as the eye could see. The remnants of campfires, abandoned ridge tents, litter, burnt out cars, empty beer cans, and discarded scooter parts covered the sludgy field overlooking the famous Dunlop Bridge. The day was damp and the campsite was like a quagmire but we loved every minute of it as we trudged around the circuit in the reddish-coloured Donington mud.

'Reservoir Mods.' The author (left) with Rawson, Chambo, Bry, Dean and Jay, posing after invading the track! Check out the crowds in the background at Redgate corner.

One of the first things we saw was the custom Vespa from the front cover of issue one of *Scootering Magazine*, and it was like we'd bumped into a celebrity. The owner must have been slightly worried as 53 strange-looking kids, wearing odd clothing crowded around his quite ordinary-looking blue PX200E! By today's standards the

The author, far left, 'enjoys' a post-rally dogburger; luckily, I survived.

SCOOTER LIFESTYLE

cover scooter 'Unknown Pleasure' would hardly get a second glance, let alone be considered for the prestigious cover of the monthly Scooterists' bible.

Despite most people getting ready to ride home after a hard weekend of partying and debauchery, the exhibition hall was still full of custom scooters and classic machines. Top scooters at the time included the *Rocky*-themed, Italian Stallion and the fantastic and timeless, Sign of the Snake (a scooter which still looks as good today, and can be seen at many custom shows around the UK). Seeing these scooters in the flesh for the very first time captured our young imaginations. The scooters were beautiful, with incredible paintwork and stunning airbrushed artwork, not to mention the sparkling chrome plating and intricate engraving.

For most of our coach party it was the closest we'd ever been to a real live scooter in our young lives, and we'd be imagining the sweet aroma of Castrol R and hearing the sounds of noisy, baffle-less scooters ringing in our ears for days to come.

Whilst we were there we also got to see some track action on the famous Donington circuit. Legends of the time: Norrie Kerr, Dave Webster, Ray Kemp, and the late 'Turbo' Terry Frankland, thrilled us with their heroics aboard awesome Vespas and Lambrettas, and we recklessly ran across the track to get to the infield during the races. These men were gods in the scooter world, and we'd seen them riding the fastest scooters ever! Sadly, I didn't get to sit on a scooter that day, get autographs from the racing 'stars', watch any of the bands (because they'd been on the night before), or see any semi-naked Scooter Girls, but it was a fantastic experience anyway.

All too soon it was time to board the coach again. Pocket money had been spent on scooter-related merchandise and t-shirts, I bought one with a picture of a scooter on the front and a Union Jack on the back and the slogan 'These colours don't run' underneath. I was too scared to wear it, though, in case I got beaten up – I never was a very fast runner and, at the time, Mods were public enemy number one with the Shadies and Casuals who hung around in Nottingham! We also got some free 'DISC '85' rally patches, and had our very first taste of a scooter rally 'dogburger'. Rally catering wasn't too good in those days and a dogburger was about as good as it got!

We arrived home in time for tea, wet, muddy and tired, but it was the day when I finally felt like

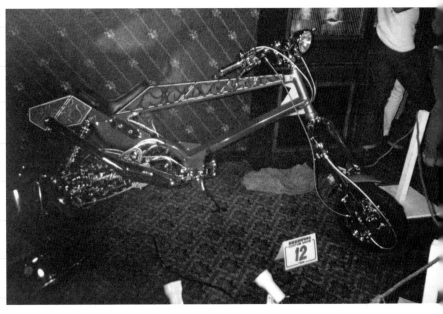

Cutdowns and chops were in vogue during the mid-eighties. Future Shock, (pictured) took customising to another level and was way ahead of its time.

Revenge, owned by Mark Wood, and Temptation, owned by Anthea Wood, are still looking this good over twenty years later. Their owners still attend most national rallies.

I belonged somewhere and, for me at least, this was where my future lay.

Incidentally, many of the lads on the coach went on to own and ride scooters (and attend a few rallies) after they left school, but, out of the 53 of us who made that epic trip to DISC '85, only a couple of us are still active on the rally scene, although

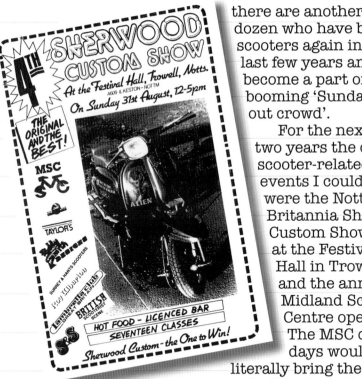

there are another half a dozen who have bought scooters again in the last few years and have become a part of the booming 'Sunday ride out crowd'.

For the next two years the only scooter-related events I could make were the Notts' Britannia Sherwood Custom Show, at the Festival Hall in Trowell, and the annual Midland Scooter Centre open day. The MSC open days would literally bring the roads to a standstill outside the old shop on Station Road in Stapleford; hundreds of scooters would pack into the small side road and block pavements, causing chaos for local residents and traffic. I managed to get my juvenile face in Scootering at one of these early open days, and a jealous mate at school put a chisel through the photo when I showed off with it in woodwork class!

In a quest to earn enough cash to buy my first scooter when I could finally get my licence in a year's time, I started to save my pocket money, got a paper round before school, and got a Saturday job, clearing tables at the local motorway services on the M1. I loved working during rally weekends at the services because we'd get dozens of scooters pulling in, and just seeing them was enough to spur me on. I spent most of my shift staring out of the windows hoping to see scooters passing through the carpark or parking up.

I was working there during the weekend of the infamous Isle of Wight riots of 1986, and the sad events of that weekend had made headlines around the country, possibly even the world. Beer tents had been set on fire, police cars overturned, stalls looted, people injured, and the scooter riders were escorted from the island in shame, and wouldn't be welcome for many years afterwards. To my mind, the bedraggled bunch of Scooterists who popped in

for a warm cup of overpriced tea during their long ride home were heroes returning from battle, and I plucked up the courage to ask a few of them what it was really like to be there.

Back in the 1980s, most rally goers were in their late-teens to mid-twenties, unlike today where middle age is becoming the norm. In a bid to keep people involved with the scooter way of life, The Old Bastards Scooter Club was launched in *Scootering Magazine*. You had to be twenty-four years old or over to join and get the coveted patch. I remember thinking, 'Fancy being that old and still being into scooters!' Little did I know that scootering is a lifelong commitment; once you're hooked it's harder to get off than heroin, and there's no rehab. One of the lads at school lied about his age and joined the prestigious club; he even started having scooter tattoos whilst he was still at school. Although his scooter riding career was over before he was 21, and he turned to cars instead, the Vespa tattoos will last a lifetime.

By the summer of 1986 I was almost 16, and I'd just about saved enough money to buy my first scooter, with enough left over for the insurance. I looked around for a machine to fit in with my meagre budget and eventually found a Vespa 50 Special advertised in the local paper. Most of my mates were buying, or saving up for, the newfangled Vespa PK 50s, but I fancied something with a bit more class, rather than the square-looking modern PK with its fancy indicators and plastic headset.

My dad took me up to see the 50 Special in Mansfield, and there it stood in its two-tone battleship grey and burgundy paintwork, it was beautiful, or it was to a fifteen year old scooter virgin at any rate, and it even had a cut down Lammy mudguard on, instead of the standard Vespa one, just like some of the scooters I'd seen at Donington the previous year. I handed over £225 (my life savings) for my pride and joy and we loaded it onto my dad's trailer for the journey home, ready to start the long countdown to my sixteenth birthday in December, three whole months away.

Luckily we lived in the countryside, and it was only a five minute push down a hill to a long, private, gravel-covered farm lane, so I was allowed to take the scooter down there and practice riding it. I couldn't understand why it kept almost throwing me over the handlebars every time I changed down from fourth to first for the downhill, left-hand hairpin approaching the farmhouse. Thankfully, somebody explained to me that you can't just slam it straight into first gear; you have to let the engine slow down a bit first! After taking on board this piece of priceless advice, scooter riding suddenly became much more pleasurable, and who knows, without it this may have been a very different story (I may have bought a Mk 2 Ford Escort when I reached seventeen). Before long I started pushing the Vespa around the corner from home and, as soon as I was out of sight, roll down the hill, drop the scooter into second gear, let the clutch out and bump start it, then ride it down to the farm.

One day the scooter started making strange noises, almost like I'd got a load of pebbles going around in the engine. Nevertheless, I managed to ride it home and my dad knew straight away that the big end bearing had gone. He soon whipped the engine out and began operating, I marvelled at his expertise as he stripped and rebuilt the complex-looking machine within a couple of days. I didn't even know how to change a sparkplug at the time (or where one went) so it was like watching a brain surgeon at work, and my pride and joy was soon back together and running sweetly again.

Within a month or so I started venturing out to other neighbouring villages on my scooter (whilst I was meant to be at the farm) and even went to the school youth club on it occasionally at night. Luckily, my parents never found out about my illegal riding (well they might do now if they read this; sorry mum) and I was never pulled up by the local village copper, PC Petford, or 'Pet food' as he was known to us. He had a fearsome reputation, and often picked on young scooter riders or lads on RD50s. For some strange reason it seemed like the village Bobbie's lifetime ambition was to make it as unpleasant as possible for anybody who rode a scooter. Ironically, this law and order and road safety Nazi was banned for drink driving a few years later, to our eternal amusement!

Legal at last on my 50 Special! Scooters were a regular sight at our school. Occasionally, there would be eight or nine parked up, often Mods and Scooter Boys from other areas would ride up at lunchtime to see us.

It was around this time that another scooter magazine was launched. Stuart Lanning brought us the first issue of *Scooter Scene* in November 1986, so we had an extra scooter magazine to buy every other month (they were both bi-monthly in the beginning). The mag cost £1.20 when it hit the shelves, and lasted until the end of 1989 when it was bought out by the publisher of *Scootering*. Stuart Lanning was taken on as editor of the magazine and eventually took over. He sold the title to Morton's Motorcycle Media in January 2003.

Finally, after the hardest wait of my life, December 11th 1986 arrived and I was allowed out on to the road for the very first time; well, legally at least. The insurance cost £49 from a local broker, and I'd bought a shiny red Centurion crash helmet for £22 – I was free at last.

My sixteenth birthday party was one of those house parties that you had to be at. It was like the party on Kitchener Road in *Quadrophenia*. My parents provided a nice buffet then went out to the Wagon & Horses across the road to let us get on with it. The invited guests started arriving with cans and bottles of booze, and I cracked open my potent barrel of 'Boots' home brew, which looked like murky sludge and tasted like it too. I'd been brewing it since I was 14 and, despite it's dishwater-like appearance,

it was soon consumed by my eager guests, as was my prized collection of miniature bottles, the cocktail came up quite spectacularly later as well!

Things quickly started getting out of hand as gatecrashers from as far away as Mansfield started turning up on scooters. Mick 'The Mod' and Pete Senneck were two names that spring to mind. Drunken, helmet-less teenagers were riding up and down the pavement on scooters and along the road two up, on the cold and misty December night. A food fight erupted in the kitchen, and rumours went around that gatecrashers were urinating in the food. To make matters worse, semi-naked girls spilled out of my mum and dad's bedroom as the 'oldies' arrived back home after the pub shut, not the best way to show I was responsible enough to take to the roads on a 'lethal' scooter. We all had a great time though, so that's all that matters, and the mess was soon

cleared up. Sadly, it was the last time I was allowed to have a party at home ...

The winter of 1986 was spent riding around with a growing group of 16 year olds who had also reached the magical milestone and could finally get their various Vespa PK50s and Smallframes out on the road. Riding a scooter was more important than losing our virginity; well, for a few months at least.

We went everywhere together, and didn't stop until the two- or four-star petrol (depending on what we could afford) ran out, or the scooters broke down, a regular occurrence at the time. Ice, snow, and frost couldn't keep us off our Vespas, and every spare penny I had was spent on new 'go faster' goodies for my beloved machine, purchased at the area's largest scooter shop, Midland Scooter Centre, a Mecca for scooter riders from around the country.

A new 'sporty' Simonini exhaust replaced the

The growing band of Notts Warriors outside the legendary Green Bogbrush, the Hornets' answer to the legendary Scooterist venue The Pink Toothbrush.

foot long piece of copper pipe with holes drilled into it which I'd fixed to my standard Vespa exhaust pipe using jubilee clips. It was the only decent thing I ever made in metalwork class, and it made my scooter sound like it was going faster than it actually was! On a good day, downhill, with the wind behind and head flat on the handlebars I'd see 40mph on the clock. I also bought a see-through HT cap which produced a colourful red spark and looked fantastic shining through the slats in my chrome Vespa side panel. It lasted for just a few miles before breaking and leaving me stranded at the side of the road. The side panel was later stolen from outside work by a local scooter-riding milkman. A flipover backrest was another great purchase, not much use, though, as I wasn't allowed to take a passenger!

A carvery chef from work owned an RD125, so I trusted him to tune the barrel of my Vespa at home. He promised it'd increase the power and make it go faster. It came back looking like he'd used the carving knife from his kitchen to reshape and hack away at my ports, and the scooter certainly wasn't any faster. Ah, the innocence of youth!

That first magical year of freedom on two wheels will stick with me forever; I rode thousands of miles with the club and various friends. Most of the mileage was done locally or on the regular 30 mile round trip to MSC for more scooter goodies but we were out and about all the time.

My furthest trip during my first year was to Cambridgeshire for a Peterborough Elite event. We'd made friends with a few lads from the club at a Midland Scooter Centre open day and they invited us to their do (a 'do' is the generic scootering term for a night-time event).

Me and a mate, Willy, set off on our 150 mile adventure with sleeping bags and a tent bungeed to the back of the scooters, my backrest finally came in useful at last! I'd carefully plotted a route using a road atlas and a length of cotton to calculate the mileage, then wrote it on a piece of paper and taped it to the headset top. I did a duplicate for Willy, so at least if we got lost we'd both end up at the same place, eventually. We had no breakdown cover and mobile phones weren't even thought of in those days, but we were young and fearless. We buzzed along for hours on our little fifties and finally arrived at the venue about three hours before the do started – an achievement in itself. As we rode into the carpark, Willy suddenly lost control of his scooter and slid

off in front of me, a second later I did the same, and that was it, our first scooter crash. Luckily, we were both unhurt and, although the scooters were a little bit scratched, they were otherwise ok. To this day I don't know what caused the crash, but can only assume it was a patch of diesel on the road.

After the do finished we were invited to stop at a local Skinhead's flat, which seemed much more appealing than pitching a tent in the dark. So, whilst dangerously over the limit (we'd probably had about four pints, a lot to a young lad), we followed Studs' much faster Vespa PX 125 through Peterborough, riding for all we were worth to avoid being lost in the unfamiliar town. We all arrived safe and sound and learnt a valuable lesson about drink driving in the process; we also had some stories to tell the lads afterwards.

Our scooter club was still going well, at one time boasting 40 members, all under the age of 18. We met at a friend's dad's pub in Alfreton and used to get a good turnout at our meetings most weeks. One particular night one of the lads pulled up around the back of the pub and a barrage of bricks and rocks were thrown over the high wall, hitting him and breaking the screen on his PK 50; a couple of the other scooters were damaged as well. The alarm was raised and we quickly jumped on our scooters and went hunting for the culprits. We soon bumped into them in the town centre; a gang of around 35 teenagers from a rival school blocked the main road through town, missiles in hand. All hell broke loose and we tried to ride through the gang but we were badly outnumbered. One of the older lads, Nick, got past the gang just as another lad decided to turn around and attack them on his own. As he performed a U-turn Nick clipped the other scooter and came off. He desperately tried to get back on his Lambretta Li 125 and bump start it as the attackers ran toward him, baying for blood. It was like watching a slowmotion replay as he ran with the stricken scooter, a machine which was hard to start at the best of times. As the gang was almost upon him the Lammy finally came to life and he managed to get away, just in time. After the adrenaline had worn off he ended up in casualty with a badly broken wrist!

Sadly, we were forced to try and find a new meeting place for the club. As we were under 18 and scooter riders were still getting a bad press we ended up using a friend's barn for the next eighteen

The Warriors at a Calverton Hornets custom show. Note the missing side panel, after the milkman nicked it!

months, until we found another friendly landlord who let us use his pool room.

As 1987 progressed I yearned to go to a proper seaside scooter rally. On rally weekends I would occasionally ride up the road to the bridge which crossed over the M1 (with a sleeping bag carefully bungeed onto the scooter to make it look like I was going to the rally), then I'd wave at the Scooterists as they rode under the bridge. Whether it was just sadness or desperation I'm not sure, but I just wanted to be a part of this exciting scene.

Local club events were happening in Nottingham

Young and reckless: from left, Nick, Raws, Martin, Jay, Docko and Corinne.

Margate 1987, the campsite certainly wasn't posh. You almost needed a scythe to carve a space for a tent in the shrubbery.

on a regular basis; the Calverton Hornets always had meetings at the News House pub in town, or at Lakeside Pavilion, a superb venue with camping facilities which attracted hundreds of Scooterists. We'd hire minibuses if we were going to events in Nottingham, or go on the scooters and camp at Lakeside; it was like a mini scooter rally. One summer evening I walked out of the do (you use this term a lot, but it's quite ambiguous) to find two Skinheads riding my beloved Vespa 50 Special around the campsite. It turned out to be a lad called John and another lad who we knew, they were only having a laugh, but it made me a bit wary of them for a while. Thankfully, there was no real harm done, and my scooter didn't have an ignition key so it was easy to steal anyway.

I had to miss the Rhyl rally, even though Willy and Rawson from school were going, I still regret it; it was one of those rallies people still talk about. Glorious weather, thousands of scooters, and the controversial ceremonial burning of the Sea Scouts' boat all added to the event, maybe not for all the right reasons, but the rally sounded like a corker. Even though I wasn't there we ended up paying for the weekend one way or another. The National Runs Committee had to raise £5000 to pay for the boat,

so we ended up coughing up on a regular basis for the next five-years. I'm sure we could have bought a fully kitted out lifeboat by the time we were done!

Later that year my wish finally came true and I made it to two 'proper' seaside scooter rallies. My first rally was to Margate at the end of July. We'd made friends with the members from another local club, 'Out of Control SC' from Heanor, They were older than us and let us travel in their back-up van. So, there I was, sixteen years old and I'm in the back of a hired Ford Transit with 15 fearsome-looking Skinheads who I barely knew. They had names like Cat, Rat, Muck, Durg, Benny and Johnny Giro. Johnny got his nickname because he was on the dole and could only afford to go out when he got his fortnightly giro. I dread to think where the other names came from, though.

We set off from the Jolly Colliers in the nearby town of Heanor at 7pm on Friday night, and followed a dozen or so 'Out of Control' scooters along 250 miles of A-roads to Kent. As learners they weren't allowed on the motorway and the journey took forever, but it was a laugh, despite being a bit cramped in the overloaded van.

We finally arrived in Margate at dawn on the drizzly Saturday morning to find more scooters than

I could have ever imagined. Smoke from campfires hung in the early morning air, and, although the site was just a large piece of jungle-like waste ground (behind Dreamlands pleasure beach), it was an awesome sight. There was an unmistakable whiff of dog shit in the air, though. We quickly put up the tents in the rain, under the overhanging trees, and tried in vain to get to sleep. However, the sound of hundreds of noisy scooters and the excitement of it all meant we were wasting our time.

After a wander around the stalls in the morning and a hearty breakfast in a seafront greasy spoon café it was almost 11am We quickly made our way to Margate's seafront pubs and were there ready for opening time. There was no all day drinking in those days and every minute counted. After the pubs closed for the afternoon we amused ourselves by playing football along the promenade, much to the bemusement of the car drivers and the large contingent of police officers who'd been drafted in especially for the event. Rallies back then were quite troublesome events, and you could be sure of a very visible police presence at every rally. Margate even had a mobile police station on the campsite and *Scootering* would boast about the number of arrests at each rally in its reports. If there had been less than twenty it was a peaceful event.

I experienced a few new things that weekend; I witnessed my first glassing incident on the campsite during Saturday afternoon, not a nice sight at such a young age, but I still managed to take a few blood-splattered photos, although sadly my old rally photos have disappeared over the years. I also witnessed the strong arm of the law as the police battered the lad responsible and then dragged him away to a waiting meat wagon. I also felt the effects of CS gas for the first time as the Kent Hotel was gassed in the afternoon (a regular occurrence back then) especially at rallies on the south coast which were popular with Skinhead troublemakers from London and Kent. You only need to smell and taste CS gas once and you remember it forever, it's a nasty chemical and it clears a pub faster than you can imagine. The victims are left disorientated, struggling to breathe, and with streaming eyes. Your initial reaction is to wash your eyes and face in cold water but the chemical can actually be rubbed into your pores and make the effects even worse, fresh air is the best initial antidote.

Times were hard in the eighties and people sometimes went to extraordinary lengths to make sure they had enough beer money to last the weekend, during my first rally weekend I watched a bloke have a whip round in the pub then drink a pint of piss, not his own either I hasten to add. Johnny Giro wasn't convinced it really was piss though, so he unzipped himself and filled the lad's glass up whilst we stood in the bar, just to make sure it was real urine. Later on as we left the pub we saw the same lad snogging a girl outside, if only she'd known. Other popular party tricks at the time involved drinking a pint of vomit for charity, eating a shit butty, blowing up a condom over your head until it burst, and the stomach churning, swallowing a chain and regurgitating it from a nostril trick. The chain would then be pulled backwards and forwards through the mouth and nose like dental floss. Thankfully many of these types of act have virtually disappeared over the years and their perpetrators have been locked in the loony bin, only to be allowed out on special occasions.

Looking back on it over twenty years later I realise that this was no place for a sixteen year old lad to spend his weekends, but it was character building stuff that's for sure, and I loved it.

On the way home from Margate we stopped at a garage, just outside town, and filled up the van and scooters. Because the forecourt was so busy, the pump was being passed down the line from scooter to scooter, and most of the riders were just riding off without paying for their fuel; there were no CCTV cameras or number plate recognition technology back then. Before we had chance to leave the forecourt the police arrived and closed the garage, one of the officers opened the back doors of our Transit and counted the bodies piled into the tiny space, you can imagine the stench that must have drifted out, you could virtually see the smell wafting out like a 'Bisto' gravy trail. Realising it meant plenty of paperwork for him back at the station he just slammed the doors and told us to "Piss off" and we were on our way.

Later on that day I got my first go on the new Vespa T5. We'd stopped at a Little Chef and the lad who'd rode around on my scooter at the Lakeside Pavilion meeting earlier in the year, threw me the keys to his lovely red and white scooter as his way of an apology. His T5 was fitted with a mark one Mikeck exhaust and it sounded gorgeous, still the best T5 exhausts ever made in my opinion. I took the scoot for a blast and was overwhelmed by the stunning performance; I knew what I'd be riding once I turned seventeen in a few months' time, who cared if it had a square headlight and a flat back end? I had been offered an original blue and white Lambretta Series One for forty quid, but decided to forget that and get a T5 instead.

My second and final rally of 1987 was to Weston-super-Mare in September; another journey in a van for me, it was a bit too far for my little fifty. This time it was an Escort van, and I was in the back with Durg, a likeable lad who had lost the use of one arm in a bike accident a couple of years before and he kept the useless limb tucked into the front of his army greatcoat, Napoleon style (strangely, a few years later his arm started working again; now that's magic!). Eighty miles from town the exhaust dropped off the van and we were forced to travel noisily at 45mph along the M5 for the rest of the journey, we eventually arrived in the early hours of Saturday morning.

After a wander around the bustling site, which was part of a council rubbish tip (I kid you not) it was time to set up the tent, or so I thought. The van driver, Mick, had fallen into a drunken sleep in the back of his van and I couldn't wake him up. So, as a last resort I was forced to spend the night with Durg under a piece of polythene that we'd found lying on the floor. We lay shivering next to a campfire until daylight; we awoke and found ourselves covered in condensation and morning dew, with burning embers literally singeing the edges of our makeshift shelter.

The rest of that weekend wasn't much better. Local newspapers and residents had opposed the event, and many of the pubs had bouncers on the doors to stop Scooterists getting in. Tesco had even removed alcohol from its shelves and had security on the door to stop us going in. The off-licences had been cleared of any booze by thirsty rally goers, so it was almost impossible to get a drink all weekend, and we ended up sharing a bottle of White Lightening on the seafront; not one of the best rallies of all time but it didn't put me off and we had quite a good laugh.

December 1987 was another major milestone for me; I turned 17 and signed the HP papers, at Midland Scooter Centre, for a brand new red Vespa T5. It cost just over a thousand pounds, a lot of money back then. Norrie Kerr was co-owner of the shop at the time, alongside Dave Webster. The well-respected Scot handed over the keys to my shiny new scooter and told me how to run it in properly and look after it. I kept my 50 Special, re-sprayed it white and sold it privately. I've often wondered if it's still around, its registration number was YCH 817Y, do you own it?

The T5 was the fastest production 125cc scooter on the road and I wasn't used to the extra power after spending a year on my Vespa 50. I thrashed my new scooter through the gears on the way home, then took it steady when I got to 45mph (the recommended running in speed), every time I pulled away the front end would lift as I struggled to master the clutch control and the ferocious blast of unbridled power, but I soon got the hang of it. My dad wasn't impressed at my running in technique, though, and bollocked me for thrashing it when we got home.

My wages for the next three years would be spent on paying for the scooter, buying 'essential' items for it (like a stereo system and waterproof speakers, for instance) and attending rallies. My paltry wages also stretched to a few engine rebuilds, which my dad helped me with. Flywheel side bearings were a regular failure on the early T5s, and it meant a strip down and rebuild. Luckily, my dad negotiated some trade discount at MSC; with the amount I seemed to spend there I was almost a trade customer! Dad could get bearings cheap through work as well, which meant it wasn't too expensive to

Tony (left), Staffy and Gary Leivers, soaked after a winter dip in the River Ouse.

keep me on the road; a good job really because I was only earning £79 a week.

I passed my part one test in January 1988 and put in for my part two as soon as possible, but unfortunately I couldn't get it done before the first rally at Easter. Back then the traditional pre-season event was put on by York SC, and it'd be a Sunday run to Knaresborough or York. I went up with the Mansfield Monsters on the cold April morning. Although there wasn't much happening, there were around 1000 scooters in the carpark in York.

The Monsters were well known for their over-the-top initiation ceremonies and high-jinks back then. As we walked back along the river, a couple of the lads, Tony and Staff, started mucking about and ended up throwing club chairman, Gary Leivers, into the freezing cold river. Gary had an expensive camera in his pocket and, even worse, he was wearing his riding jacket and had his helmet in his hand. Once he'd managed to scramble out of the cold dark water the two perpetrators went in, even Staffy who couldn't swim! Luckily all three survived and had to ride the seventy miles home in soaking clothes and soggy helmets.

The Easter weekend arrived and I set off for the Isle of Wight. I rode with the Monsters again because none of my fellow clubmates could go. Jeff Smith, President of the National Runs Committee, was a member of the Monsters and had been served with numerous High Court injunctions to stop him and the NRC going to the Isle of Wight. Quite understandably, scooter riders weren't welcome there after the rioting in 1986.

Although I didn't really know many of the Monsters at the time, a mate from school, Gray Gee, was in the club and I took him on the back of my T5; my first passenger. You were allowed pillions back then if they held a full bike licence but he had to ride for the motorway parts of the journey. This was to be my first experience of riding in a group of scooters to a rally; a major milestone.

Before we'd even left Mansfield we were pulled up by the police and told to turn back: "There's eight High Court injunctions to stop you lot from going to the island." Little did the policeman know that we had the main organiser with us, and he'd got his own copies of the injunctions in the pocket of his faded denim jacket!

One lad's exhaust fell off his Lammy on the motorway, so he tied it back on with a clutch cable. A few miles later the cable snapped and, as he tried to slow down, the exhaust bounced under his back wheel, and he was thrown onto the hard shoulder. Luckily for him he was only doing about five miles per hour at the time, so he was unhurt, but he got the piss taken out of him for a few years.

We were pulled up another couple of times before we finally made it to the ferry port but there was no way we would turn back; Isle of Wight or bust!

We arrived at Portsmouth docks, tired and dishevelled, in the early hours of Saturday morning, to find hundreds of other scooter riders waiting to board the ferry. The police were out in force, and had 'sin bins' on the quayside. Each person, back-up van, and every scooter was searched, and anything considered to be a weapon was confiscated and placed in the bins. Even items like screwdrivers, toolkits, hammers, machetes and knuckle dusters were taken and put in the bins – ok, I'm kidding about the machetes, they let you take them over so you could shave.

Boarding the ferry for the first time, with hundreds of like-minded souls, is an experience in itself. The 40-minute trip makes it feel like you're going abroad, and, as the ferry prepares to dock all the scooters are kicked into life and the embarrassing Vespa duck fart horns are pressed in unison (even though it's another five or ten minutes before the boat even comes to rest and you're left choking on the fumes). Riding off the ferry makes

The Mansfield Monsters on the 'Campsite', Ryde 1988. Danny (at the back with white jumper) is still missing in action.

the hairs on the back of your neck stand on end, it still feels great even now, twenty years since the first time I made the journey to the 'Wight isle'.

After arriving on the island, just before the sun rose over the Solent, we searched in vain for our back-up van, which contained our clothes, tents and sleeping bags, but to no avail. Our back-up driver had driven off into the sunrise with all our gear on board. I made a mental note to never allow anybody to look after my rally stuff again.

We finally found the official rally 'campsite' (a farmer's field) which was knee deep in mud and didn't look very appealing, especially without a tent, so we decided to seek an alternative place to sleep. Eventually, after riding around the island for what seemed like hours, we settled on the flat roof of a public toilet, located conveniently on the seafront in Sandown. It was absolutely freezing; early April isn't the warmest time of year for trying to kip outdoors without a sleeping bag! For the rest of the weekend we slept in a carpark in Ryde, we didn't even bother trying to put up tents on the concrete, but luckily we'd found our sleeping bags and the van so it was a bit warmer for us as we lay on the hard surface

Campsites like this one at Morecambe meant if you weren't there first thing on Friday you'd be pitching your tent on Tarmac! 'Harsh' is an understatement.

beside the scooters and watched the police arresting a couple of boisterous Scooter Boys during the early hours of the morning. Thankfully, the weather was kind to us, and we managed to have a rain-free weekend on our makeshift and very uncomfortable bed.

It makes me laugh when people complain about the harsh conditions on scooter rally campsites these days; they should have been there in the 1980s when you were lucky if the Tarmac was soft enough to hammer a tent peg into. There were no shower blocks, and no hot running water or electric hook ups back then, that's for sure. You were lucky to come home without catching dysentery!

One lad who'd travelled down with us was a rally virgin and the Monsters decided to make him feel welcome (in their own imitable style) by buying him a few drinks on Sunday afternoon. The lad, Danny, was a strapping six-footer, and they got him absolutely wasted on shorts, cocktails and pints of mild – most of them mixed together in pint glasses. He walked out of the pub as straight as a die when it closed for the afternoon, lay down beside his light blue PX 125 and fell into a deep sleep. He was still asleep the next morning as we packed up and headed for the ferry port, and we never saw or heard of him again ...

During 1988, I rode my T5 to all the national rallies and I passed my test in May. The bike test was easy back then; I literally had to ride around the block whilst the examiner walked about with his clipboard. In an effort to impress him I turned up wearing a fluorescent NCB jacket from the pit, lent to me by my dad, and a pair of heavy-duty bike boots. The test consisted of a few circuits of left turns, followed by a few circuits of right turns and an emergency stop to finish off with. Thankfully, I passed first time and was allowed to tear up my 'L' plates. The ridiculous jacket was quickly taken off and I blasted past the disgruntled examiner in a blur of green jacket and rally patches, with the stereo pumping out at full blast. I could finally take a pillion and, more importantly, travel on the motorway, so it'd be much quicker getting to rallies from then on.

I attended all the rallies that year, including the Isle of Wight, Yarmouth, Morecambe, Exmouth, Margate and Aberystwyth. Aberystwyth was a great rally, set in the beautiful rolling Welsh hills, with the campsite beside the beach. It took hours to get there, though, and a couple of us got lost in the mountains

in the middle of the night, near Ryhader. We started climbing a mountain pass which went around and around and up and up. Eventually we got to the top of the mountain and the road just started going down and down until we ended up where we'd started from. It was about 4am by this time and, of course, all the petrol stations were shut and the orange light had been glowing on my T5 for miles. We eventually ran out of fuel and, just as we were about to start walking to try and find a phone box a UFO appeared in the dark night sky, its beams of light lit up the valley and grew menacingly brighter as we prepared to be vaporised. Mercifully, we were saved, and the 'alien' turned out to be a recovery vehicle with huge spotlights, used to watch out for suicidal sheep on the lonely roads. The driver pulled up and asked if we wanted a lift! Our good Samaritan took us all the way into Aberystwyth and dropped us off at the site.

The closest rally to home was at Scarborough, just 115 miles away. We set off at 7pm on the Friday night (that was the usual time for us to set off, no matter how far away we were going) from a pub in Loscoe. Heanor John had just picked up a newly sprayed and rebuilt Italian Lambretta GP200 in metalflake red. Teething problems with the freshly built scooter meant it took us ten hours to get to the seaside; it suffered everything from snapped cables to electrical problems and heat seizures. Incidentally, the same GP is now owned by a member of our club, Snooty, and it still breaks down everywhere it goes; it must be jinxed, because it's had a complete new engine, carb, exhaust, etc., and the only time it's made it to a rally is in the back of a recovery truck.

When we eventually got to Scarborough, a favourite destination for northern Scooterists, we camped up under the cliffs on the seafront; it was cheaper than paying to get on the proper rally campsite. It was just before dawn when we pitched up and we were soon woken by an annoying chorus of seagulls who don't like to lie in on a Saturday morning. Another lesson learnt; don't camp under cliffs.

I was working full time at the motorway services by this time and having to beg people to swap shifts so that I could get the necessary weekends off for rallies, so it was time to look for another job. I'd turned down promotions at the services because it meant even more weekend work, and I eventually

The official Scarborough campsite was better suited to motocross than scooter riding and camping.

took the plunge and got a warehouse job, Monday to Friday, with only the occasional Saturday morning to work.

One Thursday night as I rebuilt my T5 for the hundredth time, ready to go to Whitley Bay after work the next day, I watched a billowing cloud of acrid black smoke over the distant fields. I thought nothing of the smoke and finished putting the scooter back together (my mechanical skills were improving and I only had a few 'spare' nuts, bolts and washers left over). The next morning as I rode to work the smell of burning got stronger and stronger. As I rounded the corner onto the industrial estate there were about a dozen fire engines outside our factory, which had burnt to the ground. Every cloud has a silver lining, though, and it meant I could actually set off for the rally in good time and get there whilst it was light and the pubs were still open for the first time ever! During the weekend a film crew arrived to film a documentary about Fred Perry. I crawled out of my tent, with last night's polo shirt on and was confronted by the cameraman. I had the hangover from hell and there was a nice pile of fresh vomit in camera shot outside my tent. I rambled on for a minute or so about why I wore Fred Perry shirts, and then crawled back into my tent. The documentary went out and my sick was still visible, they even showed the clip on *News at Ten* when Fred died a few years ago! The factory was rebuilt and my job was safe for the next fourteen

years, so it all turned out for the best.

By 1990 I was still attending all the rallies, and made it overseas for what was my first foreign holiday since going to Benidorm at the age of four. This wasn't just any overseas holiday, though, it was for a Euro rally. Myself, Jay and Paula from the Notts Warriors, set off on the carefully planned adventure to the NSRA rally in Saintes, 250 miles from Cherbourg. It took a few reels of cotton to map that route I can tell you! Ten days of scooter riding, camping, dodgy foreign food, and a scooter rally whilst we were there. The highlight of the trip was a two day stop in the lovely harbour town of La Rochelle before the rally. Many of the British Scooterists had had the same idea, and friendships for life were forged during the weekend. We even stopped at La Rochelle on the way home and dined on the finest chip, bacon and cheese butties ever made, not to mention the occasional horse steak.

The rally itself wasn't anything to shout about; the English/French rivalry led to a few worrying situations over the weekend, and one French Scooterist started waving a gun around at one stage. Another well known English lad had a nasty, drunken, scooter accident and ended up in a French hospital, with quite serious injuries and no medical insurance to get him home. 1200 miles later we arrived back in Blighty, the scooter had taken me there and back without missing a beat and the memories still live on.

In 1992 the Notts Warriors finally disbanded. We'd put on a few club dos and been on most of the rallies since leaving school, but sadly many of our most active members hung up their helmets and settled into marital bliss (a number of 'Me or the scooter' ultimatums had been issued to a few lads). The rest of the club decided to join the Monsters, myself included, and the rest, as they say, is history.

So, that's how I got started on this long scooter riding journey. I hope you enjoy reading *Scooter*

Lifestyle; hopefully, it will stir some fond memories from the past twenty-odd years. This is how I remember events, places and dates – your own interpretation or memories may be slightly different or cloudier than mine, but I'll make no apologies for that.

If you're still a part of the scooter scene or you were part of it in the late eighties and 1990s, thanks for all the good times. Whether you know it or not, you've all contributed to this book, and as long as you still live, eat and breathe scooters, you'll be making history for a long time to come. We may all be honorary Old Bastards now but the flame still burns like it did in 1983 when I first discovered this way of life. I still can't help looking around whenever I hear the unmistakable exhaust note of a classic two-stroke Italian scooter; long may it continue.

Whitley Bay was a fantastic rally; great campsite, brilliant town, and massive venue. There was usually quite a bit of violence, though, in the pubs and dos.

2 Scooter Boys through the 1980s

As the original hysteria caused by the *Quadrophenia* revival started to wane in the early 1980s, it left behind a new breed of scooter rider. Scooter Boys were as far removed from Mods as it is possible to be, the only similarity was the ten-inch wheels their scooters rode on. Gone were the smart suits, tidy scooters and fishtail parkas, and in came cut-downs, quiffs and choppers. The influence of Psychobilly bands like The Meteors, The Cramps and King Kurt, had transformed clothing, hairstyles and, more importantly, attitudes on the rallies.

Scooters had always been well looked after by the Mods, and many were equipped with chrome accessories, including the stereotypical lights and mirrors. Although these are the thing everybody remembers, they weren't quite as popular back then as you may think.

There has always been a north/south divide to a certain extent on scooter rallies. The south of the country was still predominantly Mod, whilst the northern scooter riders had gradually evolved and their style had changed throughout the seventies, and their influence was about to slowly spread south through the country.

In a bid to get rid of the 'Mod' tag, Scooter Boys revolted against everything the original Mods held dear; smart clothes and tidy scooters were suddenly a thing of the past.

As Scooter Boys took hold of the scene their

Scarborough '81 was a turning point for many Mods; they went as Mods, but came back as Scooter Boys!

24

Not having to worry about smart clothes meant eighties Scooter Boys could rough it!
Note the cutdown Vespa with welded in tank.

Cutdowns and quiffs replaced smart haircuts and chromed scooters!

'Nosferatu', a classic eighties custom ... not a home-made creation like many at the
time. Nice boots, too.

machines were quickly stripped of anything
considered unimportant. Leg shields were cut-down
to the bare minimum, or 'shaped' with a hacksaw

The new Psychobilly craze spread through the scene like wildfire.

An identity crisis for many: am I a Mod or a Scooter Boy; or perhaps a mixture of the two? Note the grass skirt, another eighties fashion faux pas!

(or even better, an angle grinder) hence the term 'cut-down'. Motorcycle fuel tanks were fitted onto a length of scaffolding tube welded between the headset and seat. Side panels were taken off to expose the chromed and polished engine, or sometimes they were cut and shaped. For the 'piece de resistance' the scooters were often hand-painted (or sprayed with cheap aerosols) in matt black, or, for a longer lasting finish, Hammerite.

Quite often, though, owners would take pride in their machines, and spend hundreds of pounds on artistic or metalflake spray jobs, and items like the flywheel cover and wheel rims were chrome plated and even engraved. Metallic, multi-coloured cable wrap was carefully wound around brake cables, and flipover passenger backrests became fashionable, replacing the old Mod favourite 'ironing board' or upright backrest. Strangely, the metal bars of the backrests were often covered with plumber's pipe lagging foam. 1980s fashion was never a strong point though; remember grass skirts and plastic policeman's helmets?

Scooter Boys had a fashion all of their own; combat trousers and bleached jeans replaced the Mod favourites of casual Levi jeans or Sta-Pressed trousers and a Meteors or King Kurt t-shirt was worn in place of a Ben Sherman or Fred Perry shirt. Army surplus clothing had always been a part of Mod culture, and green MA1 flight jackets soon caught on and were often worn with a sleeveless denim jacket over the top. Some riders even favoured leather bike jackets, which were much safer in a crash than a nylon flight jacket.

Highly polished Dr Marten's boots or shoes were also worn – ox blood being the preferred colour, followed by black – and they were a much more practical alternative for wearing on a scooter than the brogues or boxing boots worn by the Mods. Hairstyles quickly and dramatically changed, from carefully-styled sixties cuts to bleached blonde flat tops, quiffs, skinheads or horseshoes (where the head was shaved bald except for a horseshoe-shaped border which would usually be stood on end using gel – or anything else sticky enough to have the desired effect). The media tag 'Scooter Scum' was soon coined, after various seaside rallies ended in trouble and confrontation, the derogatory label often taken as a compliment.

The Psychobilly/Scooter Boy element went hand-in-hand. Scruffy and outrageous were suddenly fashionable!

Outside the Barking Smack in Yarmouth, Paddy Smith patches and green MAI jackets or denims were the norm.

The majority of mid-eighties scooter riders looked unsavoury with their scruffy 'uniform' of cut off denim jackets (worn over flight jackets) proudly displaying club back patches and the all important rally patches, which were religiously sewn on after every weekend event.

The 'Paddy Smith' patch was worn as a modern day campaign medal of honour, and was named after the Norwich-based screen printer who turned his sideline into a profitable and legendary business. Paddy started producing a few cloth scooter rally patches to earn a bit of extra beer money; little did he know how much of an impact his patches would have on the rallies. During the mid-eighties scooter rally boom it wasn't unknown for Paddy to run out of patches by Saturday morning. On at least one occasion, at Great Yarmouth, he went home and printed another load of patches, then returned to the site and sold out again. The rally patch was only available during the scooter rally though; if you forgot to buy one, or were too late, you missed out!

The 'Paddy Smith' as it became known, was (and still is) an institution, even though Paddy stopped printing rally patches in the 1990s. The modern day equivalent, printed in Stockport, is still known as a 'Paddy Smith'. Unless you'd been at the rally you wouldn't dare to wear one that a mate had bought for you, and getting your patch was the first thing on your mind when you crawled out of your leaky

Millets ridge tent early on a Saturday morning, to the sounds of a pumping stereo from the Groove records stall, which also became a rally institution.

The immortal scooter rally 'alarm clock' woke the whole campsite up with the 'classic' record *Tony Blackburn*, which was played at full blast at dawn, a great cure for your throbbing hangover! 'Tony Blackburn, Tony Blackburn, Tony Blackburn, Tony Blackburn, Tony Blackburrrn, whoah, whoah, knee Blackburn Tone ...' The annoying tune was played for a few years from the late 1980s until the early 1990s, and is still remembered with a mix of nostalgia and hatred by all the campers from the time.

The organisation of scooter rallies up until the

mid 1980s had been mainly done through word of mouth. Clubs and individuals spread the news of a rally through the scooter grapevine, or in newsletters which were produced on a battered old typewriter, then badly photocopied and posted out to subscribers. As rallies got bigger and bigger, money hungry outside promoters started taking an interest in 'our' scene and, before too long, they were putting on events to cash in.

Organised rallies were quickly growing in popularity and 'Scooter Boys' became the scourge of seaside towns around the country. Trouble was never far behind this new breed of rider, (or to be more precise the 'cling ons' who latched onto the rally scene) and although most incidents were nothing worse than a minor scuffle or inter-club rivalry, Scooter Boys were soon making the headlines for all the wrong reasons.

The rallies had gone from being a word of mouth trip to the seaside, where getting there and meeting up with other scooter riders was the main focus, to a massive gathering with live bands and entertainment, all-nighters, camping and pub crawls. Towns were being taken over by literally thousands of scooter riders, hell bent on having a good time with their new found friends, at any cost.

Teenage exuberance led to confrontation, arrest and wanton vandalism and destruction, including the infamous Isle of Wight riot in 1986 and the well publicised burning of the Sea Scouts' boat at Rhyl in 1987.

The National Runs Committee had taken a vote a few months before the Isle of Wight event and ruled that no outside promoters would be used to organise the campsite. Chris Burton of Torch Promotions was already planning to put on all-nighters, and a few bands over the weekend, but he had problems

INVASION!

Barriers go up at Smallbrook Stadium

SMALLBROOK STADIUM **CLOSED** WATER SUPPLY CUT OFF, & TOILETS REMOVED.

● **ABOVE:** They shall not pass. The barriers and the notices go up at Smallbrook. Security guard Peter Gray is pictured on the gate before the start of the island scooterist invasion. — Picture 7250-2.
BELOW: Preparing the new rally camp site at Northwood. Promoters Mr. Chris Barton (right) and Mr. Tony Class. — Picture 7253-1.

getting an entertainment licence on the island unless he agreed to take over the running of the site; so that's what he did. As a result, the NRC issued newsletters advising affiliated clubs to boycott the site and find alternative accommodation.

At the time it would usually cost £1 to camp for the weekend on a rally, the entrance fee for the infamous 1986 bank holiday weekend was a whopping £7. Beer prices were another bone of contention and the price of a can of warm beer on the site steadily crept up over the weekend to peak at £1 a can. Scooterists don't like to feel ripped off, and the choice of bands over the weekend didn't help matters. As well as the usual headline acts, like Buster Bloodvessel (who was the guest compere for the weekend) and the late, great Edwin Starr, the promoters had also booked a few 'Oi' bands, including The Business, Vicious Rumours, and Condemned '84. Although the bands weren't strictly right-wing, they helped to draw plenty of right-wing Skinheads and hangers-on to the rally, and the atmosphere soon turned sour. After the bands had finished the crowd decided to

Cars were an even worse problem on scooter rallies in 1986 than they are now. Many of the occupants weren't interested in scooters. At the Isle of Wight, tension boiled over with horrific results.

Bare chested revellers sport bloody scars after rioting on the campsite. In the background an upturned catering wagon burns and gas bottles explode.

get a bit of revenge for the over-priced beer, so the beer tent was robbed and set on fire. The caterers were attacked and some of the other stalls looted, and police and fire officers were pelted with missiles when they arrived on site. The event soon made headlines around the country. It's worth noting that, although there was a large Skinhead presence at the rally, there were just as many ordinary Scooterists

Back-up vans were searched by the police, but many Scooterists had already passed out after sampling the stolen hooch. It wasn't just outsiders causing trouble at this event, although they provided a convenient scapegoat!

St. Nicks' car park at Yarmouth was always packed with a sea of scooters.

involved in the riots as there were Skinheads, and many club back-up vans returned to the mainland laden with bottles of stolen beer.

Apart from mindless vandalism, fighting, and inter-club rivalry, scooter theft was also a big problem, and anybody caught at it would be dealt with severely, indeed. The stigma would live with them for a lifetime; once a scooter thief, always a scooter thief.

One of the favourite rally destinations at the time was Great Yarmouth. The police would set up roadblocks at a small petrol station just outside the town and check that the scooters were 'legal' and that riders' documents were in order. 'Producers' would be issued to anybody without a licence, MoT and insurance document, or for any minor vehicle

defects. You had seven days to take your documents to your local police station and, if they had found anything wrong with your scooter at the roadblock, you also had to have it repaired and get an MoT station to stamp the form before visiting the cop shop, or you'd be prosecuted.

It's still highly debatable whether the police were acting illegally or not, but nobody kicked up a fuss at the time, it was just a natural part of the rally. Other towns, like Margate and Whitley Bay, also carried out roadblocks.

St. Nicholas' car park in Yarmouth was the usual rally campsite, the seafront grass and Tarmac ground was one of the best sites on the scooter rally calendar.

Other towns would put us as far away from

tourists as possible, often on an unsuitable and unhygienic piece of wasteland, but in Yarmouth the council was quite happy to have us (or, more to the point, our money) and we were given a prime spot right on the seafront, just opposite the pleasure beach (incidentally, where Madness filmed the video to *House of Fun*). The site would be rammed to bursting point with thousands of scooters and a sea of multi-coloured ridge tents; there were no dome tents back then. The scooters were parked in a separate 'Scooter safe area'. The safe area had been pioneered by Jeff Smith in 1983, in a bid to cut down on the number of scooters and parts being nicked, but in Yarmouth the local council ran the area and you could leave your scooter in relative safety for the weekend for just £1: about the price of a pint of beer. It cost a fiver to camp as well, then there was the cost of getting into the evening events, so rallies weren't much cheaper than they are today, and people had much less disposable income in those days.

There were no washing facilities on site, other than a few dodgy portaloos, which you wouldn't dare enter after the first day. The thought of a mountain of pooh, mixed with gallons of stale vomit and a cocktail of urine didn't bear thinking about, and it was always a good laugh for somebody to tip the portaloo upside-down whilst you were in there. I've seen (or rather smelt) the after-effects on a lady who had been in the wrong place at the wrong time, and it wasn't pretty, I can tell you!

Back in the 1980s most people didn't bother washing during a rally – an extra spray of deodorant would sort you out for the weekend – but then the invention of wet wipes and the fragrant Kentucky Fried Chicken wipes transformed scooter rally hygiene overnight. If you could find somewhere to freshen up (or make friends with some posh Scooterists in a B&B) it was a bonus. My favourite freshen-up place was McDonald's, in towns that had one of the fairly new burger bars, that is. I'd get there for 8am, just as it opened for the day, and do my business in a clean toilet and have a warm wash.

At Great Yarmouth, a public toilet across the road from the site had decent washing facilities; you'd pay the attendant ten pence and be able to have a wash with hot water, brush your teeth, and use the relatively clean loo ... heaven!

Tiffany's nightclub at Yarmouth became a legendary venue, and the right-wing attack on Ska legend, Desmond Dekker, on stage at the venue is still talked about over two decades later. It helped to escalate tension which had been bubbling away for a while, and led to a decade of trouble between the left- and right-wing factions, as well as with ordinary Scooterists caught in the middle, with friends on both sides of the political fence.

As with any scene where differing groups of people come together to get drunk and have a good time, there is always going to be a certain amount of friction, and 1980s scooter rallies certainly had their fair share of problems. Scooter rallies have always attracted a diverse group of people. Everybody is slightly different, be it in the clothes they choose to wear, the music they prefer, or the type of scooter they ride. You can like heavy metal, Oi, Punk, Northern Soul, Reggae, Ska, Two Tone, Indie, House, Dance, Rave, or hate music altogether, but as long as you love scooters and are prepared to enjoy yourself and can stand people taking the piss you'll fit in nicely. You can be an opera-loving transvestite on the scooter scene but, as long as you ride a Lambretta, you'll still be treated as an equal! It really is a place where boundaries can be crossed between people of all persuasions, social classes, age and wealth. A forty-year old millionaire will happily rub shoulders with a twenty-five-year old shelf-stacker.

During the eighties people weren't quite so tolerant, though, and political differences caused the majority of problems. The right-wing, neo-Nazi Skinhead element began to grow steadily, brought about because of the recession, increasing levels of immigration, and boredom. Although many of the right-wing people on rallies also had a love for scooters, as well as extreme politics, there were also plenty of them who just came along for a fight. They'd turn up in cars and vans and, before long, there would be trouble in the pubs and dos. Frightening and ferocious levels of violence ensued from both sides, and from other Scooterists who had no interest in politics but loved the scooter scene, and didn't like the troublemakers spoiling things. At one stage football hooligans were even recruited to get involved.

The atmosphere at rallies soon began to change for the worse. Pubs were wrecked in mass brawls and CS gas was sprayed into venues and bars. Before long people were sick and tired of having to watch their backs and take sides against friends

Name IAN GRAINGER
Address
D.O.B. 11.12.70
Membership CS490EF

and acquaintances. The majority of rally goers just wanted to have a good time and the constant hassle made quite a few good committed Scooterists think twice about attending events. The arrival of the rave scene was another nail in the coffin of the scooter rallies, youngsters who had become disenchanted with the problems on the rallies soon latched on to this exciting new dance movement and rally attendance suffered as a result.

To try and restore order, the National Runs Committee decided to bring in controversial new ID cards, everybody had to be a member of the NRC and have a card with their photo on before they were allowed into the night time dos. The idea was to frighten off the 'cling ons' and hopefully bring some normality back to the rallies.

The card system wasn't a popular move, and neither was the idea of stopping bands from playing. The plan was to get rid of people who only wanted to come along to see a band or to cause trouble. Although the move was heavily criticised at the time, both ideas were necessary and, although it didn't cure all of the problems, things did take a turn for the better – for a while at least.

During this time 'pirate rallies' began to spring up which didn't help matters, some were in direct competition with the NRC and would be held in a different part of the country, whilst other promoters were there to provide an alternative to the main do at a rally.

VFM was one of the main alternative promoters. 'Value For Money Promotions' was set up by Scooterists Nick Jolly of Junction 13 SC and Kev Lowe from Notts Britannia SC. VFM would play alternative music which often wasn't catered for by the NRC. Music by bands such as The Smiths, The Cramps, The Cult, Dexy's Midnight Runners, Stiff Little Fingers, and party tunes from the likes of Gary Glitter would keep the alternative Scooterists on the dance floor all night long. Not many of us would like to be in Gary Glitter's gang these days, though.

VFM usually hired a small venue or, more often than not, a pub in the rally town, and people who either couldn't get in to the NRC do or who preferred the VFM style of music and its relaxed door policy would go there instead. Staunch NRC supporters thought the alternative dos were there to undermine the official rally organisers' efforts, but, nevertheless, the pirate events continued throughout the late-'80s and early-'90s. Little did they know that, just a few years later, the alternative VFM dos would become the main rally entertainment, and smaller promoters would occasionally put alternative events on in rally towns. How times change!

Scooterboy World

Although the Scooter Boy phenomenon has died down to a certain extent and the majority of rally goers dress in a casual manner these days, there are still a hardened few who will do all they can to preserve the 1980s 'scooter scum' image. Many of these modern day Scooter Boys can be found on the popular website and forum at www.scooterboy-world.co.uk. I asked Nik Skeat, the creator of Scooterboy World to tell us what possessed him to unleash Scooter Boys on to the world wide web.

"Write a few words about Scooterboy-World.com," he said. "Hmm, not easy, as it's not really something I've reflected on over the however many years it's been running, but let's start with the web page that leads to the forum, I think this covers where we come from:

The original Scooter Boys may not be quite as prevalent as they once were, but it's still an honour to be considered 'scum' to many.

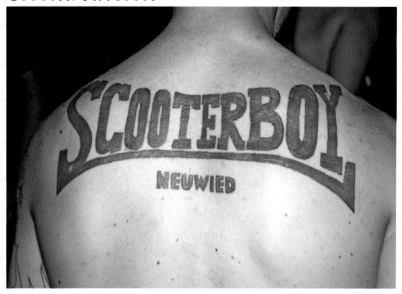

Scooter Boys have spread to other parts of Europe, as demonstrated by this German Scooterist.

"If you are easily offended, are a Mod, a restoration anorak or an eBay rip off merchant go and find another forum. We really don't want you in here unless you can post without any attempted trolling. Scooters are for riding. They aren't for polishing, thread counting or making a profit from. They're a fun way of getting around the country – oh yes, if you make a point of doing scooter rallies with your scooter in the back of a van, or worse, on a trailer hitched to a Chelsea tractor then piss off now. Not just from here, but from the scooter scene. Thank you.

Tattoos and facial piercings may make people look aggressive, but often they're the nicest people you could ever wish to meet.

"Sometime around 1997 I finally discovered the internet and did what most people do when they first logon ... I went searching for websites that interested me. The porn sites done, I then went looking for scooters, and the rest is history. Well it would be, it's in the past.

"A succession of forums caught my eye in the early days of my surfing – the original LCGB one with its Sunday night chat, then the forum known only to those who used it as 'The Orange One' as none of us can remember its name 10 years on. From there the growing band of scooter loving web users moved on to the original Scooter-Forums.com when it was run by a Scottish gentleman known only as 'Ace'.

"Around this time, myself and one or two others were getting a little disgruntled with the, shall we

Mohicans, chains, tattoos and piercings; and that's just the girls!

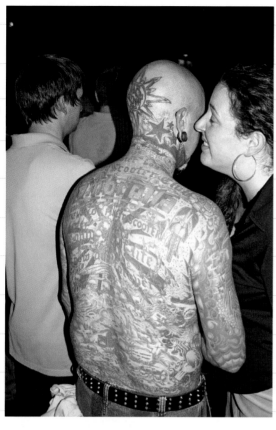

This Scooter Boy from Whitby is covered from head to foot with tattoos.

say, 'backward-looking' aspect of the scooter scene, whether it was those who complained loudly that "Li150s from 1963 never came in that particular shade of white", the "bolt on every bit of chrome tat you can find to slow it down a bit more" Mod revival revivalists, or the 'born agains' who wanted to take the scene back to where it was when they left it in whatever year it was; arguments that can still be found in some corner of the internet – but not ours.

"We were looking for somewhere that catered for those, like me, that had started their scootering career in the early to mid-'80s, and had never gone too far away, somewhere that accepted everyone as long as they were prepared to use the scooter for what it was intended; riding.

"I'd realised prior to this that the scootering sub-cult that had boomed around those years was the forgotten youth culture that no-one outside of us diehards remembered; Scooter Boys. As far as Joe Public was concerned, if you rode a scooter you were a Mod. That's right; dreadlocks down your back, or a foot high mohican, a leather jacket and tatty oily jeans, you were still a Mod! Time to put the world to rights then? I hoped so.

"It was about this time that Ace's original Scooter-Forums.com vanished from the web, I'd acquired a book on web design (which I'll finish reading one day!) and so the idea of Scooter Boy World was born. Originally, I'd planned on creating

a history of the Scooter Boy from the early '80s right through to now, with a small forum attached, for the thirty or forty remaining Scooter Boys that I thought were still out there.

"Somehow I got sidetracked, and the forum has become arguably the busiest English language scooter-related forum on the web, and the site hasn't been touched for about three years!

After plugging the new forum on every other forum I could find, and armed with what for a British site were a couple of novel ideas – accepting autos as a part of the scooter scene was a very early one, and the scam-busting eBay section – SBW (as it quickly became known) was born.

"My original estimate of around 40 members was passed in the first month, and as I write we have had over 1700 memberships, though in recent years this has been subject to an annual cull of inactive accounts, and the number currently stands at around 1000, with members from all around the world. I think I was slightly pessimistic on the score?

"We've always tried to foster a club feeling, with scooter parts being sold, often at a fraction of what they would cost on eBay and the like, technical help coming from many members, including the several shop owners we've had on board, and experienced custom scooter builders aren't slow in coming forward with suggestions and help.

"It's not all been plain sailing, though, we were booted from one forum host due to our anything goes attitude to posting, and got threatened with the same by the next.

The third forum I managed to crash due to my lack of knowledge, but the current forum has survived for something like four years, without the hosts catching us doing something we shouldn't. It's only a matter of time, though ...

"SBW has never strayed too far from its roots and beliefs. Scooters are not ornaments for the back of your van, or an investment to be polished before being ridden once a month if it's sunny. They're a cheap and cheerful form of transport, capable of getting you where you want to be if you're not in a hurry. The social side of the scene is of paramount importance to us, although we've constantly changed to reflect the changes in tastes. Who would have imagined 10 years ago that small rallies in a field, once the preserve of bikers, would be the most rapidly growing area of the scooter scene?

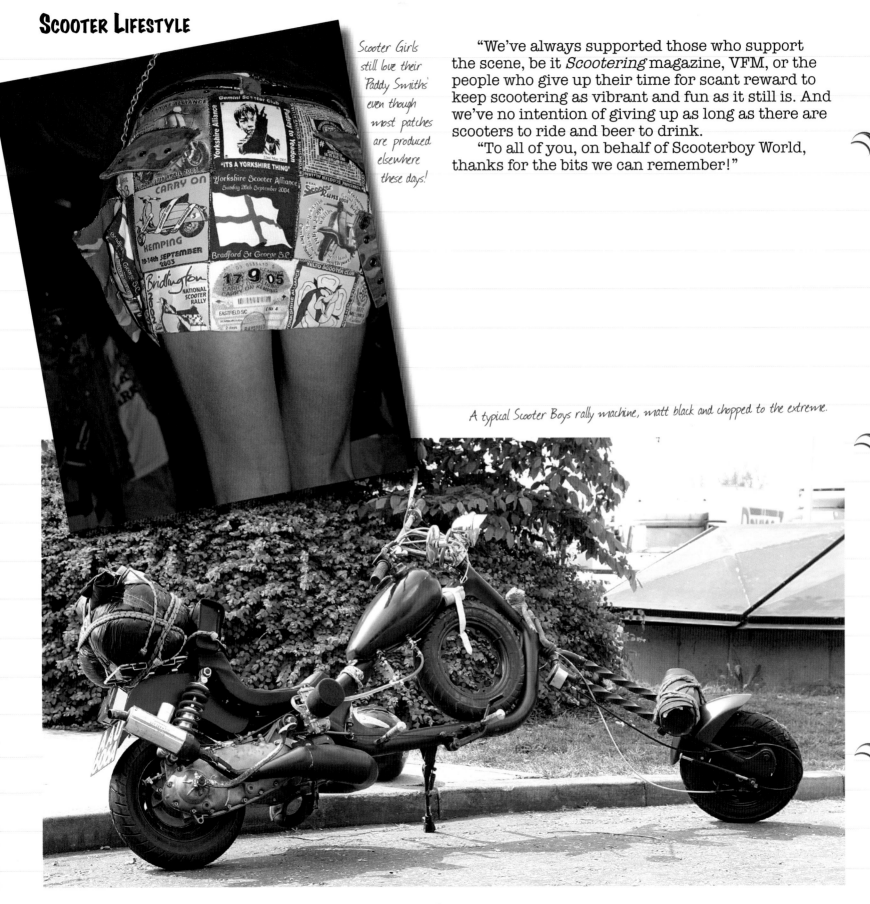

Scooter Girls still love their 'Paddy Smiths' even though most patches are produced elsewhere these days!

"We've always supported those who support the scene, be it *Scootering* magazine, VFM, or the people who give up their time for scant reward to keep scootering as vibrant and fun as it still is. And we've no intention of giving up as long as there are scooters to ride and beer to drink.

"To all of you, on behalf of Scooterboy World, thanks for the bits we can remember!"

A typical Scooter Boys rally machine, matt black and chopped to the extreme.

.3 The twilight years

In the early-'90s, the fascist/left-wing clashes were still happening on a regular basis. 'Blood & Honour' Skins were still common on rallies, and tensions ran high at most events. More often than not, though, it was ordinary Scooterists who attacked first, or provoked the Skins into fighting in a bid to discourage them from attending rallies.

The term 'Blood & Honour' was in reference to the sewn-on patches Skins sported on their black Alpha MA1 jackets, and the name of a right-wing alliance which was set up in 1987. It was also the name of a record by leading right-wing band Skrewdriver.

Running battles were fought in the streets at popular rallies, including Aberystwyth and Morecambe. Evening events were attacked, and people from both sides were injured at rallies and club events around the country.

In 1992 it all came to a head in Margate. A firm of right-wing activists came down from London for the weekend, intent on causing trouble, or possibly with a view to putting an end to the violence once and for all. During Saturday lunchtime a pub was attacked, and a number of people on both sides were injured. Calverton Hornet member and future VFM front man, Steve Foster, was badly hurt, leaving him scarred for life. Later that night the venue was also attacked, the main doors were locked and barricaded from the inside whilst people fought on the terrace outside, overlooking the sea. At least one person was thrown over the cliff edge and another battered with a scaffolding pole. The battle raged as the right-wing tried to force the doors open. CS gas was sprayed into the building and people choked on the noxious fumes inside.

Fearing an attack, Scooterists inside the venue started smashing up furniture to use as weapons, but eventually the fight lost its momentum and things returned to normal, or as near to normal as a do can get after a mass brawl and a CS gas attack! I'm not sure why the fighting came to an end, I was one of the people inside the Lido complex where the event was being held but, thankfully, it was soon over. Many of us left the Lido that night with heavy wooden chair legs concealed inside our flight jackets; just in case. It was a long and

Bare chested right-wing Skinheads often sported tattoos declaring their allegiance to various bands and political parties.

Sieg Heil! Poses like these were a regular sight on mid-eighties rallies. Many Scooterists became disillusioned as a result of the constant hassle.

The NRC became known as the NSRA, or National Scooter Riders Association. Jeff Smith was still the President, and a regular committee sat beside him at the annual number ones meeting. The meeting would be held during December or January to decide on the coming year's national rally venues and dates.

The meetings were long, drawn-out affairs, with plenty of arguments for and against various rally towns and dates. The Scottish contingent always put up a good argument as to why there should be more rallies up north, and I always admired their commitment, often travelling for 250-300 miles before they'd even left their own country. A weekend away for them

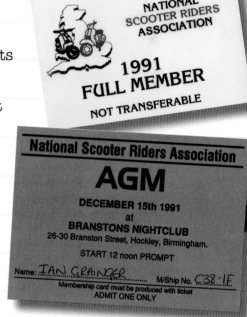

frightening walk back to the campsite that night, and an uneasy atmosphere hung over the rally for the rest of the weekend. Skinheads were targeted and threatened on the Sunday, most of them just innocent rally-goers with politics that didn't fit in, and the majority of trouble-causers from the previous day had wisely disappeared.

The problems of the late-eighties and early-nineties started to gradually disappear after the battle of Margate, and the number of black flight jackets with the telltale celtic cross badges and patches being proudly displayed dropped significantly. It would be a few years, though, before the rallies would recover and friendships would overcome political differences.

Rally attendance started to drop dramatically during the mid-nineties. Some people left to buy houses, get married, or sample the new rave scene, whilst others were simply disillusioned with the scene as a whole. The ID card system was still being criticised by many, but it was a necessary evil, to a certain extent, and it certainly made it harder for troublesome people to get into the events.

A typical mid-nineties NSRA rally at Santa Pod. The events weren't very well attended, but gave Scooterists a chance to try the 1/4 mile 'Run what you brung' on the drag strip.

wanted a scooter rally in the 1980s, but with perseverance and a fair amount of charm Jeff gradually managed to win them over. The lack of attendance, trouble, and back-stabbing took its toll, though, and he eventually retired his position after Bridlington that year, never to be seen or heard of again, in scootering circles at least. Even committee members who'd been with Jeff for over a decade were dropped from his life. This was a bitter end to the NSRA, and a sad way for Jeff to leave; after all, he fought long and hard to keep the rallies going during some very difficult times, so we owe him our gratitude for helping to preserve the scene.

A new organisation soon rose from the ashes of the NSRA. The British Scooter Riders Association was formed by a few individuals and rally promoters who had an interest in putting on major events, without one person or organisation taking overall control. The BSRA involved clubs and Scooterists who were willing to put on national-sized rallies, capable of attracting over a thousand people.

VFM, which had up until this time been a 'pirate' organisation, only interested in putting on alternative events, was also involved, and the new regime helped breathe life back into the stale scene. The original VFM promoters had been replaced by ex-Calverton Hornet Steve Foster, and Stockport Crusader Johnny Bolland, and, before long, they were putting on many of the major scooter events, and bands were being reintroduced for the first time in years (apart from the NSRA's last stab effort at Southport, where it put Dodgy on shortly before the organisation folded).

As the twentieth century came to a close things were starting to buzz once again, people who had dropped out during the bad times dusted off their old scooters, or bought new ones, and started to get involved again. Many were amazed to find people they'd known ten years earlier were still involved, and things had only changed for the better. The word went out that scooter rallies were back in business, and slowly but surely the attendance on rallies began to increase.

could easily be a 1000 mile round trip. Scooterists from the south west of England also showed 100 per cent commitment, and travelled thousands of miles to attend events all through the season; the Modrapheniacs and the Troglodytes are two southern-based clubs worthy of mention.

After the meeting, affiliated clubs and individuals would send off their membership forms and photos to get the all important NSRA cards for their members. Many hangers on invented bogus club names and gave false details to get their cards, often just as a poke-in-the-eye to the unpopular rules.

A couple of weeks before the rally, a newsletter would be sent out naming the town for the forthcoming national run. Locations weren't revealed too far in advance, though, in an effort to stop troublemakers finding out where we were going. The secrecy wasn't popular, but in a way it added to the excitement as you waited eagerly for the newsletter to drop through your letterbox, never quite knowing where you'd be going until the last minute. Rumours would go round as to where the rally might be, but the scootering grapevine wasn't as good as it is these days; internet forums and mobile phones make it much easier for gossip to spread than in the pre-digital days of the 1980s and 1990s! The secrecy made it tricky for many people trying to book time off work, though, so the inevitable Friday afternoon 'sickness' became the norm for many.

By 1997, Jeff Smith was becoming increasingly bitter at the scene. He'd put a lot of work into making scootering an acceptable proposition again, and had built a lot of bridges with local councils and police chiefs. Hardly any town in the country

4

The dawn of a new era

The end of the twentieth century signalled an upsurge in interest in the scooter way of life. Even as recently as the dawn of the new millennium, Friday night dos on a pre-season rally would attract only around 60 people. Times were about to change, though.

Friendly faces greet you at every event.

The scooter cult has survived for over forty years. It's had its good times, and its share of bad times, but the true Scooterists have been there through it all. When times were tough they stuck together, forged long-standing friendships, supported events, and kept the flame

The modern scene offers great live entertainment.

burning, and without this core of regulars the scene would have simply fizzled out long ago. Thankfully, though, it's risen like a phoenix from the ashes. Not only has the scooter scene thrived in the United Kingdom, but it has also spread across Europe, America, Australia and the Far East, where regular rallies and events take place each year, often attended by British riders. The scene has never been as vibrant, well attended, diverse and harmonious as it is now.

Nothing can run perfectly all the time, though,

'Johnny Rotten' plays to the camera.. Tribute bands are a regular fixture at many rallies.

The modern Scooterist often dresses in stylish but practical riding gear. Armoured jackets will prevent painful gravel rash in the event of an accident.

and in 2007 it was problem after problem for rally promoters in the UK. It was the wettest, most miserable summer since rain was invented, and this led to problems for many rally organisers. A number of events were threatened with cancellation, or subjected to disruptions and technical difficulties by the weather. Venue closures and council ignorance also caused countless headaches for rally organisers. If it wasn't one thing it was another.

The Easter rally at Scarborough was one of

If hard partying is more your style, events like Holiday in Holland provide the perfect place to abuse yourself for a weekend!

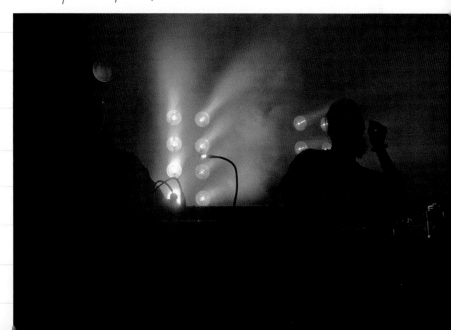

SCOOTER LIFESTYLE

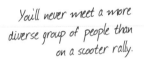

Another Scooterist takes to the stage to entertain the crowds.

These days most events are friendly. People are there for a good time.

the first to suffer, and was almost cancelled after the seafront venue for the evening dos was found to be unsafe during structural works. Thankfully, the management and VFM worked around the

You'll never meet a more diverse group of people than on a scooter rally.

problem and another room was provided. The rally went ahead in glorious sunshine and the popular Yorkshire town was packed solid with Scooterists all weekend.

Lincoln Scooter Club, the organiser of Sticky Rock in Skegness, also had problems with bands letting it down, as well as terrible weather during the weekend, which left at least one family without a tent or any belongings when they returned to the site in the middle of the night. The kind-hearted organiser immediately called a taxi for the family and put them up in a top hotel for the night, at a cost to the club of £180.

Margate was

The right-wing Skinheads were overtaken by original Skins, lovers rather than fighters!

another rally which could have gone pear-shaped. The local council bowed to pressure from residents living near to the proposed campsite and, at the eleventh hour, told VFM that it couldn't use the site (cynics amongst you may wonder if the local elections, which were scheduled for the week after the rally, may have had something to do with the council's decision). An emergency 500 mile round trip to Kent by the VFM organisers resulted in a new site being secured and the rally-going ahead as planned, albeit in a very tired and run down-looking town compared to the one we had last visited twelve

years before. Needless to say, we won't be going back there in a hurry, unless the much-needed and long-overdue regeneration of the once-popular town takes place.

The rally at Cleethorpes took some careful thought and planning before it could go ahead. The original venue, the Winter Gardens, was closed unexpectedly in January 2007, and it took the organisers three trips to the seaside town before a suitable replacement venue could be found (a campsite called The Beachcomber). The date had to be brought forward by a month to fit in with the venue's calendar. Once The Beachcomber

was secured the organisers came under fire from fellow Scooterists for changing the date, because accommodation and days off work were already booked. Things took a turn for the worse when the council told the organisers that they couldn't have the campsite they had originally been promised. Another trip to the town secured an excellent new campsite one mile from town, with a cheap bar on site and loads of space on the football pitches for camping. Because the site was a bit out of town, coaches were laid on (at a cost to the scooter clubs of almost a thousand pounds) to provide free transport into town and down to the do and back on Saturday night.

The terrible weather also caused problems at the Cleethorpes rally. Torrential rain flooded the town during the Thursday night prior to the rally. The Beachcomber caravans were flooded, as was a neighbouring caravan site. Murky, brown water lapped at the doorsteps and electricity boxes of the caravans, and holidaymakers were evacuated

Cleethorpes turned out perfectly, despite all the hassle beforehand.

SCOOTER LIFESTYLE

from the sites by boat. Many Scooterists who had booked into caravans for the weekend were left with nowhere to stay when they arrived at the campsite on Friday afternoon! Thankfully, both venues being used for the evening dos were unaffected by the rain.

The weekend stayed fairly dry, the town was as busy as ever, and things went pretty much to plan. The only problem during the weekend was created by idiots on the coaches. Despite the coaches being free, there's always a few dickheads who will spoil things for everybody else. At the busiest time of the night, people were literally fighting to get on to the coaches outside the town's most popular pub, The Bootlegger, and one of the coach drivers was hit by a so-called 'Scooterist' (and I use the term loosely). Quite understandably, the three coach drivers returned to their HQ in Grimsby at 10.30pm and refused to drive again.

A swift decision was made by the organisers to try and sort things out, because there were still 500 people trying to get from town down to the do, and almost 2000 people would be stuck at the venue at 2am trying to get home again – things could easily turn nasty. Myself and Matty from the Mansfield Monsters (who co-promoted the rally with the Olympics SC), went down to the coach depot on a desolate industrial estate and managed to sweet-talk the coach company into resuming service. We had to agree to provide stewards to man the coaches, to avoid any further incidents.

We eventually got back to the do at midnight, and club members were hastily put on the coaches to provide security. The venue was rocking and everybody had a great time – apart from us that is!

All the Scooterists were collected from town and taken home again at the end of the night without any further problems.

It's not an easy task trying to keep 2000 drink-fuelled Scooterists happy, but the organisers of our national

The change of venue at Cleethorpes gave the event a welcome boost.

scooter rallies do everything in their power to make things run as well as possible.

The largest event to suffer from a cancellation was the Run to the Shires in July. 2500 Scooterists were planning to make their annual trip to the popular event at its new venue at Catton Hall in Weston on Trent, Derbyshire, but the worst flooding in British history meant the rally had to be postponed just four days before it started.

The rescheduled Shires rally turned out well, despite the late September date.

Local roads leading to the campsite were flooded, the campsite itself was under a foot of water, and many other parts of the country were also severely affected. 350,000 people in Gloucestershire were left without water and electricity as a result of the monsoon-like conditions, which had been with us pretty much non-stop throughout June and July. Sheffield was also badly hit, and a dam threatened to burst and flood the busy M1 motorway. Hull and many other parts of Yorkshire were also badly hit, and inland cities across the UK even had to use Coastguard helicopters to evacuate stranded workers from office blocks, and to airlift motorists to safety.

The rescheduled event finally took place during the last weekend of September, and the days leading up to the weekend were very wet. Persistent heavy drizzle on Friday meant the ride to the rally was a damp one for most but, thankfully, on Saturday, the sun came out and the event attracted over 2000 happy Scooterists. The rally had a festival vibe to it, with a huge big top type marquee for the main entertainment venue and a lovely view across open countryside and the River Trent, which flowed alongside the campsite.

Live bands, acoustic guitarists, alternative cabaret artists, and even a solo set from talented ten-year-old Matt Cummins, all added up to a fantastic event. Dozens of stalls, caterers, a beer tent, custom show and kid's entertainment outside meant the rally goers made the most of the late summer sunshine, and the weekend was a complete success. Every cloud has a silver lining!

The only thing to dampen the atmosphere at the Shires was the unfortunate death of Nottinghamshire Scooterist, Tom Fletcher, who collapsed and died shortly after arriving at the event. Valiant efforts from a trained paramedic and the St Johns ambulance couldn't save him.

If the weather wasn't causing enough trouble, the newly introduced smoking ban came into effect on July the 1st 2007, and immediately put a spanner in the works. The ban has made it harder and more expensive to police events. Imagine 1000 people in a venue trying to go in and out of the building every half an hour for a cigarette and you'll understand how hard it is to enforce, especially

Dad and his lad; the future will be provided by our kids.

It's always nice to see fresh-faced youngsters enjoying the scene and living the lifestyle.

Brit Pop, and clubs like Brighton Beach have brought a number of new people into the scene.

at venues without enough outside space to accommodate the high number of nicotine addicts and their friends who come out to chat. The smoking ban has had quite an impact on rallies so far; take a quarter of your punters out of a venue and the atmosphere changes considerably. As with any change it takes a while for people to adapt and I'm sure before too long things will settle down again and get back to some kind of normality, especially at cold or wet events where the temptation to stand outside isn't quite as appealing as it is in the height of summer – on the rare occasion when the sun actually shines on a weekend, that is.

2007 was a trying time for rally organisers, but against all the odds most events managed to run in one way or another. It's easy for punters to judge and criticise events when things don't run as smoothly as possible, but it takes a lot of time, effort and stress to organise a successful event; often the only reward being the satisfaction of seeing a packed dance floor and a town full of scooters and scooter riders enjoying themselves amongst like-minded people.

The scene has learnt from the mistakes and problems of the 1980s and 1990s, and most people have grown older and wiser as a result. Although there's not an abundance of teenagers coming into the scene, there are still newcomers appearing on a regular basis. Often, the youngsters who do come along are the teenage offspring of Scooterists who have been nurtured and brainwashed from birth on a diet of Vespas, Lambrettas and good living by their devoted parents.

We can also thank the 1990s Brit Pop explosion for revitalising the rallies. It suddenly made scooters fashionable again, and brought these iconic machines

into the public eye once more. We always knew we were cool, though, and didn't really need some spotty little Herbert pop star with a publicist in the know to tell us scooters were the things to be seen on! The effect of Brit Pop may not have been as dramatic as the *Quadrophenia* revival in the late 1970s, but it provided a steady influx of new scooter riders who have carved a name for themselves on the scene and helped to rejuvenate it once again.

The scooter rally calendar gets busier and busier each year. As well as the established favourites, like Bridlington, the Isle of Wight, Woolacombe, Mersea Island, Kelso and Cleethorpes, there are plenty of regional rallies and events which run every weekend from March through to November. Winter used to be a quiet time as far as rallies are concerned; five months of rest between the last one in October and the first event at Easter. Nowadays, though, even if there's no national event on there will undoubtedly be a club do, parts fair, alliance event, or maybe even a foreign rally, custom show or do to attend. As a result, the scene runs non-stop

British and American Scooterists come together in Vegas 2003.

for 52 weekends of the year; there's no rest for the wicked or party hungry Scooterist now, and living the lifestyle is a time-consuming, tiring, and very expensive pastime.

If you're not content with doing rallies throughout the summer, there are also plenty of other events through into November, as well as the occasional overseas winter trip.

VFM and the South West Scooter Clubs have successfully taken over 500 Brits to Las Vegas for a long weekend of collaboration and partying with the American Scooterists. The first big trip to Vegas in February 2003 gave us the chance to drink the bars dry in the Riviera Ballroom, and sample the casinos and bars of downtown Vegas.

The British contingent (in true Scooterist tradition) spent four days sampling most of the bars along the famous strip, getting married by dwarf Elvis impersonators, and fighting with knife wielding cowboys (I kid you not), and long-lasting, trans-Atlantic friendships were formed as a result.

The Scooter Girls get prettier as well.

The trips to Vegas in 2003 and 2005 were surreal, to say the least; imagine arriving at Manchester airport and finding that the departure lounge is full of familiar faces and good friends from the scooter rallies. Our flight was the busiest, with 326 Scooterists on board, and ours was just one of the UK flights. There were over 200 more Scooterists from England, Ireland, Scotland and Wales at various other airports, not to mention our American cousins who were loading trailers with scooters to cover the vast distances between different parts of the States.

We arrived in Vegas after a connecting flight from Atlanta and almost twenty hours of weary travelling. Many of us were looking forward to getting in to bed. Things didn't quite go to plan, though. As we walked into the Riviera Hotel at 2am (our base for the long weekend) we found the bar packed with the exact same people with whom we socialise back home. One quick drink before bed turned into an

Rockabilly is becoming more apparent on the scene again.

all-night drinking session, and we finally hit the sack at 6.45am, only to be woken up by an alarm call at 7am for a day-long helicopter trip to the Grand Canyon!

The highlight of Vegas for me was DJ'ing on the

Every rally town is full of your best friends, old and new.

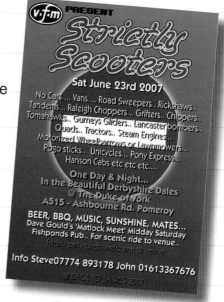

to The Kaiser Chiefs or The Who, The Jam, Secret Affair, Frank Wilson, Paul Weller or Angie Stone. Classic rally tunes can be in the charts today or they can be forty-years old, and every one could become an anthem, a song that will always remind you of a certain town, person or place on a rally. It doesn't matter where you're from, what you do for a living, how old you are, or how long you've been there, the rally scene holds no barriers. Barristers and City traders mix with printers, factory workers and nurses. Old meet young, and the old never get older, Scootering is the key to eternal life, health and well being. A true Peter Pan society.

VFM has also organised social events to Tenerife for the past couple of years. The Spanish island is much closer than Vegas, of course, and attracts masses of party hungry Scooterists with the promise of a bit of winter sun and great times by the sea. Although these events are well supported and make an ideal winter break, Tenerife isn't the

Saturday night with my partner in crime, Matty. A thousand Scooterists from opposite sides of the Atlantic, who share the same love of scooters but who lead very different lifestyles came together on the dance floor and sang their hearts out to British classics, including the patriotic Angelic Upstarts record, *England,* and the legendary sing-along football song, *Vindaloo.* One American remarked to an English Scooterist afterwards, "You guys are crazy, but who is this Vindaloo guy you all love?"

It doesn't matter where in the world you go, a scooter rally still has the same buzz and the same characters that make it such a special event. There's nowhere else like it; the sense of comradeship, loyalty and the whole buzz of being there isn't the same on bike rallies, VW rallies, raves, festivals, or anywhere else for that matter. There's no greater sight than a floor packed with sweaty dancers, who range from sixteen to seventy-five, all dancing and singing along

Holiday in Holland was always a favourite Euro rally.

European scooters favour the street racer style, with plenty of trick parts and engineering.

kind of place you can easily ride to. However, there are plenty of scooter rallies throughout Europe that attract Scooterists from the UK and which are close enough to ride to.

Holland has been a favourite destination, partly because it's so close but also because it's a liberal country where people can relax and see a few sights

Passport control in Rotterdam at 8am after the overnight ferry from Hull.

SCOOTER LIFESTYLE

that you don't get to see in dull and dreary Morecambe! Holiday in Holland is one of the best attended foreign events, known for its friendly atmosphere, old school scooter rally feel, and all-night music policy. It's been a favourite amongst British, as well as French, German, Austrian, Dutch and Belgian scooter riders. Sadly, the annual event has outgrown itself in recent years, a victim of its own success, and alternative overseas rallies have taken its place. Hopefully, one day it will be resurrected.

Great Britain may be the place where scooter rallies and the lifestyle which surrounds them started, but the bug has spread throughout the world. Every country in Europe has its own thriving scene, always on a smaller scale than in the UK, but they still live the same kind of lifestyle; although, as you'd expect, the Brits are still the best binge drinkers in the world!

It seems as if the whole universe is tuning scooters, customising them, racing, riding or attending rallies at home and abroad on small capacity Italian machines. Even countries as far apart as America, Thailand, Australia and Japan have their own events and clubs – you name a country and it will almost certainly have a scooter scene of its own. It may have a slightly different format and focus than the British scene it emulates, which is still predominantly based around the pubs (with a scooter ride thrown in to get there) but the overseas Scooterists are a welcome addition to this thriving scene.

There has never been a better time than the present to get involved with the scooter lifestyle, whether you're looking for mates to ride around with on a Sunday or a club to travel to Belgium, Italy or Austria with, you'll be able to find something to suit your own personal scooter way of life, and you won't need to go too far to find them.

A few years ago we were as far underground as an Arthur Scargill convention, hated by the media and general public alike. These days we're welcomed into children's hospitals at Easter, with our chocolate eggs donated by riders on toy runs. Almost every other advert on television, in magazines, on billboards and in newspapers carries the image of a scooter. Pop stars and television personalities ride them in their videos and around London, often catching the lens of the paparazzi photographer in the process. Seaside towns welcome us with open arms, thankful for the millions of pounds we bring to the local economy every year, whilst the majority of ordinary British tourists seek guaranteed sunshine abroad.

Many venues at popular seaside rallies struggle to cope with the numbers trying to get in. A Friday night do can often attract 1800 Scooterists, and Saturdays are occasionally ticket only affairs – lose your ticket and you'll struggle to get in. If the numbers keep on rising it won't be long before rallies start attracting ticket touts!

Our scene has almost become mainstream, but it's still controlled from within by well-established, long-term scooter riders, who will do everything in their power to make sure events continue to be run by 'proper' road-going Scooterists, as opposed to outside promoters eager to cash in on the scene we have all helped to protect and nurture into the greatest social phenomenon in youth culture, ever. We may not exactly be over-run with youths these days, but we're all still young at heart, and the thrill of riding under-powered shopping bikes will help us to find the secret of eternal youth – long may it continue.

The Isle of Wight

To get an insight to the way a modern scooter rally runs there's probably no better place to start than at the largest scooter event in the whole world. The Isle of Wight has always been a Mecca for Scooterists; it may only be a short ferry trip from the mainland, but psychologically it's almost like going abroad. Many Scooterists making their first trip to the island have been tricked into taking a passport with them so they could leave the mainland! Oh, how we laughed.

After the rioting and problems in 1986, the islanders and authorities weren't really friendly towards us (and who can blame them?) so we kept away. However, the NRSA, just before it folded, decided it was time to go back to the island. Although attendance wasn't great, the rally went well, with no trouble, and paved the way for what was to become the largest scooter rally in the world.

Every year, the August bank holiday weekend sees up to 10,000 Scooterists from around the world converging on the island. The rally has become legendary amongst Scooterists; loved by many and hated by some regular rally-goers largely because of the thousands of 'part-time' scooter riders who only ever attend this one event, often travelling only a few miles from their homes on the south coast, or, worse still, taking the scooter there in a van!

As you ride down the motorway towards the ferry port at either Southampton or Portsmouth, you'll see literally dozens of vans and trailers loaded with scooters, which will be unloaded at the ferry port for the owners to ride on to and then off the ferry. Then they'll pose for another four miles into the centre of Ryde, whilst riders who have travelled hundreds of miles by scooter to get there secretly laugh at and pity the 'van boys'.

Blatant van boys will even take their loaded van onto the island and unload the scooters at their luxurious hotel or on the campsite, along with gazebos, patio furniture and gas barbeques, whilst 'proper' scooter riders with oily hands and dirty scooters look on in disgust from their humble and well-used rally tent.

Riding your scooter there is all part of the buzz for most 'proper' riders. Scooters may not be particularly fast, and tuned scooters

will drink more petrol than a Ferrari, and probably suffer some kind of mechanical mishap, but you can't beat the excitement and exhilaration of riding with a group of your best friends on what is essentially a glorified shopping bike! You'll be white lining and slipstreaming all the way to keep your speed up as much as possible, and, although the top speed isn't usually much more than 70mph, you'll feel every bump, pothole and cat's eye on the road, which makes the experience feel much faster than it actually is. Who needs a superbike when small wheels and dodgy handling will make your scooter feel like it's doing 150mph?

When you've ridden with a scooter club or group of mates to events up and down the country for a number of years, you learn how each of them rides. You can anticipate when they're going to overtake, and be ready to pull out, either before or after them, without letting those precious revs off and be left facing a long wait for the power (if that's what you can call it!) to build up to a reasonable cruising speed again.

You'll also know when your mates need to stop for fuel. Lambretta TS1 riders can have as little as 50 miles between fill ups, depending on whether they have a long range tank fitted or not. Malossi-kitted Vespas can usually do around 65-70 miles to a tank, and a Vespa GTS can run all day; well, almost, but they

White lining: the only way to travel to a rally, leave the cars and vans at home!

Nothing beats a ride to a rally in the sunshine with 20 of your best mates.

in a fiver, names are drawn out of a crash helmet, and whoever draws the name of the rider who breaks down first wins the cash! You're gutted if you draw the name of a GTS or standard Vespa rider, but you'll be rubbing your hands together if a tuned Lambretta comes out of the hat!

Don't worry if you break down because, as long as you've got a group of mates to take the piss out of you whilst you're stuck on the side of the road in the rain, with oil all over your hands and tools strewn around you, everything will be fine. Also, whether your stricken scooter gets there on the back of a breakdown truck or in the club back-up van, you'll be happy to know that one of your clubmates has just made £50 out of your misfortune!

As the group gets closer to its weekend destination more and

will do around 110 miles to a tank and, compared to a TS1, they'll need less than half the petrol to fill up for the same mileage.

Most petrol stops end up taking half an hour or longer. Somebody will start tinkering with their scooter, trying to find an often imaginary sound they've 'heard', whilst others will decide to have a cigarette or nip into the services for food or the loo, just as you're ready to set off again!

A 200 mile journey should theoretically take around four hours but, when a group of scooters are involved, it can easily take nine hours or more (perhaps the 'van boys' have it right after all).

A convoy of scooter riders will usually consist of a few kitted Lambrettas, a standard PX 200, a tuned Vespa, a bog-standard Lambretta SX200 or GP200, and, more often than not these days, a couple of Gilera Runners, Italjet Dragsters or Vespa GTSs. Each type of scooter has its own limitations and, apart from the modern four-stroke scooters, there's always a chance it'll break down, or at least rattle a few nuts, bolts and fillings loose along the way.

Our scooter club runs a sweepstake to see who'll break down first. Before every rally each rider puts

A five minute fuel stop can take an hour or more when travelling in a group!

Lambrettas often get a bad press; I wonder why?

they were a bit dismayed when the 'Scooter Scum' returned.

Hundreds of smartly-dressed Mods would take over the centre of Ryde. The lads would wear flash suits with flamboyant sixties-style shirts, and their outrageous bouffant haircuts would turn heads amongst the Scooterists present, never mind the general public who couldn't help but stare at these strange-looking but very stylish people. The girls wore sexy mini dresses, leather boots, and had equally outlandish hairstyles. The Mods used venues of their own for their night time entertainment, so the Scooterists would only bump into them in town during the daytime and before the dos started.

The old rivalry between Mods and Scooterists was only ever friendly banter between two opposing scooter-riding factions, but, after witnessing the way modern Mods dressed and acted, the piss taking began and, eventually, after a few years of us being back on the island the main Mod organisation (the New Untouchables) decided

Another packed ferry prepares to leave Southampton.

more scooters start appearing on the road, at garages along the route, or parked up in lay-bys having a breather (or more often than not with the panels off and the toolkit out fixing yet another problem).

Excitement starts to build as you see the distance signs counting down to the ferry port. More and more scooters join the road at every junction and, when you arrive at the docks you're greeted by hundreds of scooters all hoping to be allowed onto the next available ferry.

So far we've neglected the Mods, mainly because they have their own separate scene these days, but they are an important part of our history and many Mods still attend national rallies. During the years when Scooterists weren't welcome on the Isle of Wight, the Mods adopted the island and carried on the tradition of holding an annual August bank holiday rally there, and

RED EAGLE

enough was enough, and they abandoned the island so that they didn't have to mix with the comparatively scruffy Scooterists. The New Untouchables now visit another favourite Mod haunt during the bank holiday weekend instead – Brighton.

Although many of the most outlandish Mods have deserted the island, there are still a growing number of Mods who make the annual pilgrimage. The two factions, Scooterists and Mods, seem to live beside each other these days and enjoy their own different events without any friction; just how it should be.

Hipshaker is the main Mod do on the IOW, whilst VFM uses the massive, 3000 capacity Planet Ice Stadium for its main events. There's also a large do at the Ryde Theatre, and various other promoters put on smaller events over the August weekend. These cater for all musical persuasions, from Skinheads and Soulies to Mods and Scooterists.

The modern Isle of Wight scooter rally is the premier event of the Scootering season, and literally thousands of Scooterists from the UK, Ireland, Belgium, Spain, France, Germany, Austria, Italy, and other parts of Europe (and even as far away as the USA) descend on the ferry ports of Portsmouth and Southampton for the annual trip.

Foreign visitors are a common sight on the island. Riders come from France, Belgium, Austria, Holland, Italy, and Germany, and there's even the odd American or two.

There's not much room for your luggage on a chop, but they're usually comfier than they look!

Smallbrook Stadium is the true heart of the Isle of Wight rally.

The weekend starts early for many Scooterists. A Thursday afternoon ferry means they can get over to the island without having to pre-book, and then either check into one of the hard-to-get-hold-of bed and breakfasts, which are usually booked a year in advance, or they can book on to a public campsite.

Kite Hill is a favourite site where 500 Scooterists will usually camp and enjoy 'proper' washing and toilet facilities, as well as a quieter night than can be had on the official VFM scooter rally campsite at Smallbrook Speedway Stadium.

The VFM site is located around three miles from Ryde town centre, and, while it may not be posh, it's where the atmosphere of the rally is generated. By Thursday evening there will be around 800 early arrivals, already camped up at the stadium, enjoying a free welcome barbeque and a disco in the club room, whilst watching speedway racing on the adjacent track.

The scooter rally traders begin to set up stalls on the infield after the racing finishes (or earlier if there's no meeting taking place) ready for the rally to start officially on Friday morning.

As the venue closes for the night, scooters are still arriving, and tents are being set up by the fluttering headlights of scooters ticking over noisily on the field.

As the first ferries of the day arrive on the island,

You can buy pretty much anything on the campsite. Around 50 traders set up to ply their wares.

Arrivals get more and more frequent throughout the day.

The site soon begins to fill up.

Umbrellas become makeshift parasols as the temperature soars!

the steady stream of scooters quickly becomes a flood, and the atmosphere starts to build for another Isle of Wight International Scooter Rally.

It's all hands on deck as the VFM stewards welcome each new arrival to the site with a goodie bag and rally itinerary, as well as the all-important wrist band, which proves you've parted with your £15 to camp for the weekend.

The scooter gods usually smile on the Isle of Wight, and we're treated to beautiful sunshine almost every year. The campsite gets busier and busier as the day goes on, by early afternoon literally hundreds of scooters disembark each and every ferry, whilst hundreds more wait to board. Forget to book your crossing and there's every chance you'll be waiting for hours to get over to the island.

From dawn till dusk the traders ply their wares and you can buy everything you can think of, from scooter parts and accessories, to T-shirts, rally patches and exhausts. You can even have the resident artist airbrush some custom artwork onto your scooter side panels. If you had an 'eventful' journey, you can have your scooter repaired whilst you wait.

The site is a hive of activity throughout the day; early arrivals will either be chilling out in the campsite bar, or on the balcony which overlooks the campsite, or just sitting on the grass by the tents, chatting and having a laugh with old and new friends from around the country.

During the afternoon many Scooterists will venture into Ryde to visit their favourite pubs, whilst other Scooterists prefer to spend the day posing on their scooters up and down the seafront in a seemingly endless circuit, or sitting on the grass opposite the King Lud, watching the world go by.

Chilling out involves fixing scooters in the sunshine.

Friends and acquaintances arrive and are greeted with the kind of welcome reserved for your nearest and dearest, and that's what they are. You've grown up with these people and been through good times and bad, they're as important as your own family, even more so in some cases. These friends have been with you through thick and thin, you may only see some of them at a scooter rally or club do every few weeks, but close friendships have evolved as a result.

The inevitable weddings, affairs, children and divorces happen, and one way or another the intimate rally scene means we've probably all slept with one another at some stage; if somebody

The grass on Ryde seafront will be full by Saturday afternoon.

Posing around Ryde is all part of the fun, and people-watching is a favourite pastime for many.

was to spend time researching the scooter rally 'relationship tree' the result would be frightening!

As evening approaches it's time for people to drift off to get themselves ready for the first proper night of the rally. Campers will be forced to endure

Lifetime friendships are often forged on scooter rallies.

the muddy floor of the communal showers on the campsite, or, if they're a bit clever, they'll nip into town by scooter and go to the local swimming pool for a refreshing dip and a hot shower before getting ready; perfect.

Whatever your musical persuasion you'll find something to entertain you on the Isle of Wight. The VFM do is the main choice for the ordinary rally-going Scooterist. Live bands and top scooter rally DJs in the main room play everything from indie and Brit Pop to Ska and soul. There's even a bucking bronco at the side of the dance floor which is great fun after a few pints! There's a small but adequate Northern Soul room

VFMs finest DJs spin an eclectic mix of scooter rally favourites. DJs Evo and Daz only have eyes for each other, though!

upstairs, and the smell of talcum powder hangs in the air as the Soulies shake it around to help their leather-soled brogues slide gracefully across the lino-covered floor.

The 1400 Scooterists who venture into the do on Friday night are guaranteed a top night of entertainment. An ice stadium might not be the kind of place where you'd expect a hot night but, once the dance

The 1400 or so Friday night revellers enjoy tribute band, The Clone Roses.

People pack the site on Saturday, and it's chaos at the gate for those coming and going.

floor starts to get busy, the steam starts to rise from the covered ice and an eerie mist floats at waist height, enveloping the revellers.

Trying to find a venue large enough to cope with a scooter rally is easier said than done and, although the ice stadium isn't a perfect place to create a party atmosphere, it is the largest venue on the island, and the only one suitable for the busiest nights; Friday and Saturday.

After a bit of pushing and shoving to get on the coaches after the do finishes, its' back to the campsite (or B&Bs for the lucky ones) where the hardiest party people stay up drinking, smoking and talking absolute rubbish until daybreak!

A dawn chorus of noisy scooters arriving from the early morning ferries wakes all but the deepest sleepers, the baritone exhaust note reverberates across the sun-baked earth and penetrates your throbbing head – there are no lie-ins on a scooter rally campsite, and hangovers hurt!

Saturday is the biggest day on any scooter rally and the Isle of Wight is no exception. Hundreds more scooters pour onto the island from both ferry ports throughout the day. The campsite gets busier and busier, and all hotel rooms on the island (within a taxi ride of town) are full to capacity.

Early morning bargain hunters try to get around the dealers for the pick of the rare secondhand parts.

The show is the most prestigious on the scooter rally calendar and attracts a wide variety of machines, including this unique Lambretta Series 2 and VW sidecar!

From 11am the custom show is in full swing inside the ice stadium. Around 80 of the finest custom scooters in the country (and even a few from abroad) battle it out for prestigious trophies and the chance of a cash prize. Gleaming chrome, sparkling paintwork, and fantastic artwork adorn almost every machine in the room. As well as full-blown custom scooters there are chops, cut-downs, and well-engineered scooters with auto engine conversions. Fully restored 40- and 50-year old

scooters, which look like they've just rolled off the Italian production lines, sit side-by-side with rat scooters sporting matt black paintwork, and 'styling' courtesy of the angle grinder.

Whatever style of scooter floats your boat, whether it's a moddy style machine, embellished with lights, mirrors and enough bolt-on goodies to double its weight, or a tidy Vespa street racer with a race replica

It's not often you see a Puch Alpine, but at the IOW in 2007 we were treated to this fine pair.

As you'd expect at the Isle of Wight, Moddy-style scoots are quite popular in the show.

paint job and highly-tuned engine, you'll find it in the Isle of Wight custom show.

Many custom scooters are ridden to the rally and hastily cleaned by the owner as he (or she) sets up their display at the show. Afterwards, they are ridden out and back to the campsite or B&B, and then, ultimately, home again. To some, the scourge of many rallies are the owners who won't actually ride their scooters, and the Isle of Wight is the worst event on the scootering calendar for this; the 'curse' of the 'van boy' strikes again! Custom scooters arriving in vans are a very contentious issue amongst owners who spend hours on a show morning polishing every nook and cranny to remove all traces of road dirt.

Elsewhere in Ryde, the pubs are full to bursting point with Scooterists, and they overflow on to the pavements and bask in the late August sunshine. The seafront is packed with Scooterists, pint in hand, just enjoying watching the poseurs riding up and down the promenade. Many Scooterists prefer to ride around all day rather than relaxing with a few beers.

The grass opposite the King Lud is chock-a-block, and will be until late afternoon, whereupon people slowly disappear to get changed for the evening. The ever-popular Wetherspoons, Sports Bar, Marine and Crown are full as well. Even the local tourist board has started to promote the Isle of Wight rally. The seafront tourist train sports posters advertising the

It's standing room only by mid-afternoon.

badges and coasters can be bought in many of the shops along the main shopping street leading up the hill out of town. You can't blame them for trying to cash-in on one of the largest events of the year, and, with an estimated £2 million being spent by rally goers over the weekend there's money to be made for the entrepreneur.

Saturday night is the big one; well-known

scooter rally, and shops fill their window displays with souvenirs aimed specifically at the Scooterists. Target posters, scooter models,

Whatever style of scooter you like, you'll see it in Ryde during the August Bank Holiday.

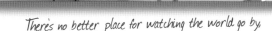

There's no better place for watching the world go by,

tribute bands play at the VFM do and Ryde Theatre, both venues catering for a slightly different audience, but all with a common bond – the humble scooter. Up to 1800 people will be at the VFM do on Saturday night, and a good few hundred at the New Untouchables event and Ryde Theatre, not to mention the various smaller dos and pub discos. Many people prefer to stay on the campsite, or at a pub close to their bed and breakfasts, or just

A pretty Modette chills out astride her Vespa.

Right: The sights are often quite breathtaking, and can make even the most unpopular models of Lambretta seem attractive!

As the sun sets people begin to drift away to get changed for the biggest night.

The Isle of Wight

A gorgeous SX 200, Extra 'S' Type soaks up the last of the sun's rays.

Ladies strut their funky stuff in the Hipshaker marquee.

Hipshaker attracts the Moddy crowd, and a few beautiful ladies as well!

The ice begins to melt at the VFM do.

do a pub crawl around town. It's almost impossible to estimate the actual number of scooter riders on the island because they're spread out everywhere.

There are also a lot of Scooterists who use the Isle of Wight as an annual family holiday, they'll book onto an ordinary campsite, perhaps even hire a caravan, and either have a quiet night on the site or maybe go into town for a while. Some parents will even bring their offspring to the do. This is frowned upon by many who prefer to keep their social life separate from their children (or haven't got kids of

Mods play air guitars outside the Ryde Castle.

their own) and wouldn't risk bringing their delicate children into a potentially dangerous environment.

Mix almost 2000 people with enough alcohol for a brewery owner to retire, and there's always the chance of an accident occurring, or a fight breaking out, and a small child being crushed. The consequences don't bear thinking about. Over the years I've witnessed a few incidents at other rallies, including a ten-month-old child being left

A scooter rally attracts all kinds of people, and you can be forgiven for forgetting which decade you're in!

to sleep inside a huge speaker stack at the side of the stage whilst the band was playing. On another occasion, a family left its young kids in a tent at the Burton Brewers rally, one five-year-old girl was found wandering around the pitch black campsite at 1.30am, crying for her mum. Once the parents were found tempers ran high, and it was only the swift intervention of others that saved them from a good hiding from irate Scooterists.

Thankfully, these days trouble is only an occasional problem and it's usually nipped in the bud before it gets out of hand. Most Scooterists know each other, so there's a mutual respect between them, and the security is provided by ordinary rally-going Scooterists who give up their time to help keep things in order. These Scooterists are into the scene just like anybody else, but a large proportion of their

The VFM roadcrew are all active Scooterists, and their bark is usually worse than their bite.

weekend away from home will be taken up with helping to organise and run the rally.

On most rallies Scooterists take care of virtually everything. They man the gate at the campsite, provide, clean and service the portaloos and mobile shower blocks (yes imagine yourself cleaning those after a long weekend!) pick up all the litter from the site, sort the traders out before and during the rally, organise the custom show and trophies, arrange PA and disco equipment at the venue, which quite often involves dismantling it all and moving the heavy gear to more than one venue over the course of a weekend.

Scooterists also DJ in the venue, provide security, take money on the door, and carry the risk if anything goes wrong. They also have to listen to people whinging about how expensive it is to get in or how crap the band/DJs were on the way out. With such diverse musical tastes you could never please all the people all of the time, and prices have hardly risen in the past fifteen years, despite increasing costs to put events on.

Whilst most people just come away to enjoy themselves, the organisers and staff spend much of their time away either working or trying to stay relatively sober for their shift later that day or night. Spare a thought for the people who work until the last person has left the do at 2am (or even later at some places, including the Isle of Wight) then have to be up at 7am to set up the parts fair or work a gate shift on the campsite, and then stand and listen to people moaning all day. Remember that the people you're moaning at are the reason you're there; the rally organisers may make money from most of the events

Teenage offspring of existing Scooterists often grow up with the scooter rally way of life, and will become the next generation. Younger children should be left at home, though.

they put on, but without them there would be no national rally scene.

Over the last few years, legislation has crept in which makes it more expensive and harder to put on scooter rallies. The recent Security Industry Authority legislation has meant that a scooter rally (or any event in licensed premises) has to have a certain number of registered security staff working.

Up until recently, organisers could get a few mates to work the door for a bit of beer money and free entry into the do, but the new SIA regulations mean that trained door staff and security have to be used. Up until 2005, most venues would allow you to use a couple of their bouncers and a few stewards, but nowadays a venue can be closed down if it's paid a visit by the local authorities and is found to have less than the recommended number of badged security.

As a result, VFM, Lincoln Scooter Club and the Mansfield Monsters paid to send some of their helpers and club members on the SIA course in 2006, at a cost of over £400 per person. This means scooter rallies and events can still be run using fellow Scooterists to provide most of the security, although most venues still insist on using at least two of their own door staff as well.

Despite what you may think, the local bouncers can be useful because they know who the idiots are from their own town and can point them out and either stop them getting in or make the other stewards aware of them. Often it's outsiders coming to dos that creates a problem.

Using Scooterists to keep an eye on things inside the do can often prevent a problem before it arises, or help to defuse a potentially volatile situation. A friendly word with an aggressive Scooterist is often well received from a fellow scooter rider, whereas an enthusiastic bouncer may escalate the problem.

Another modern and vital cost of putting on a scooter rally is public liability insurance. The 21st century 'blame culture' means that even small club events should be covered by public liability insurance. A slip on a dance floor could (and has in the past) resulted in a very expensive lawsuit for whoever booked the venue. There are a few clubs around the country who have endured the stress and despair of receiving a solicitor's letter regarding another Scooterist who has injured themselves at a rally or event and decided to try and make a few quid out of the unfortunate accident. As a result, some Scooterists have almost lost their homes trying to pay the massive legal bills and fight the unnecessary action. Thankfully, we in the UK don't experience problems like they do in America, not yet at least, but don't even consider putting on a large event without adequate public liability insurance. As a plea to Scooterists as a whole, if you do injure yourself whilst you're drunk or mucking about, please just put it down to experience and take it on the chin, or one day this litigation culture might well kill our scene!

After a couple of days of hard partying on the island many Scooterists wake up on Sunday morning and, for one reason or another, decide to go home. By lunchtime the once crowded campsite at Smallbrook Stadium is decimated, as over a thousand tired rally goers pack up their canvas homes and load the scooters ready for the long and tiring ride home.

There's one last stop for them before they head

Packing up on Sunday is a lazy affair.

Early arrivals get ready for the largest scooter ride out in the world!

for the ferry port, though; the world's largest scooter ride out. Masses of scooters converge on the ice stadium car park at lunchtime, ready for the massive procession to begin. Flanked by police outriders, a solitary scooter at the front will be kicked up and, like a Mexican wave flowing through the car park, the other scooters suddenly burst into life, followed by a cloud of environmentally unfriendly blue smoke.

Thousands of tourists, spectating Scooterists, and hundreds of locals line the promenade with cameras and camcorders at the ready as the police bikes lead the procession out of the car park and through the town, running red lights and forcing cars to stop along the way. As you move slowly out of the car park the hairs on the back of your neck tingle as a thousand camera flashes hit you and the onlookers cheer the riders on, you suddenly realise that you really are a part of something very special. In 2007 the ride out broke the record for the longest unbroken procession of scooters in the

The Ice Stadium car park is filled to capacity in time for the ride out.

It only takes one scooter to start up and a few thousand others join in!

world, the official figure was 1132 taken as an average, the count was 1599 but a few cars managed to get in-between some of the scooters, so the lower figure has to be submitted. Whether it's accepted by the officials at *Guinness Book of Records* or not there's no doubt that this is the largest gathering of scooters in the world. Take into account the fact that only a small percentage of scooter riders on the island actually take part in the ride out and you'll begin to understand just how massive this event is. Official ferry company figures often top 7000 scooters during the weekend

The ride out usually ends up on the other side of the island at the Rugby Club in Sandown. By the time the first scooters arrive there the last ones are still leaving Ryde! If you stand in one place and watch the procession, it will take forty-five minutes for the scooters to pass by. Remember that there are probably five times as many scooters on the island as there are on the ride out. Many owners either can't be bothered to do the ride out or are busy shaking off the previous night's hangover, and are getting ready to sample the 'Sunday Club' instead. This really is the largest scooter event in the world!

The traditional bank holiday Sunday Club is one of scooterings best kept secrets. There are only four of them a year (not including the Christmas period) so they're pretty special, and, whilst most rally goers prefer to get home and have a night in their own bed and a day to recover before going back to work on Tuesday, the Sunday Club is out for what is arguably the best day of the scooter rally.

Pull up and admire the procession; it'll surprise you just how big this event really is.

If you only ever do one scooter ride out in your life make it this one; it will bring a tear to your eye, guaranteed.

For many of the organisers, DJs, stewards, traders and staff, Sunday is the first day that they can relax. Most of the hard work has been done and it's time to let down what little hair they have left. The meeting point will be decided on the day before, and everybody will meet in the chosen pub at around noon, dressed and ready for the long day ahead. There's no getting changed for the night time; this is a proper, long, hard, binge drinking session which will probably last for fourteen hours!

Nobody ever claimed a Scooterist's life was a healthy one, and a doctor would be alarmed if he realised just how hard a scooter rally is on the body. A three or four day bender, very little sleep, and a diet of fatty rally foods (or in many cases no food at all) aren't likely to do you much good. Thankfully, many of us live a healthy lifestyle away from the rallies.

The use of recreational drugs is quite common on the scene, as it is in any town, village or city in the country. Mods favoured amphetamines in the 1960s, as did Scooter Boys in the '80s and early '90s. These

For a minority the lure of the traditional Sunday Club is more tempting than a ride about on a scooter, especially when there's well over 200 miles to ride the next day!

in the country will have its fair share of recreational drug users, and they won't need to lie, cheat or steal to fund their lifestyle. It's a fact of life.

Complacency and familiarity with their surroundings means Scooterists often forget that what they're doing on a night out could land them in prison. At the Isle of Wight in 2007 one lad was even caught snorting coke in the toilets – whilst the amazed management and cleaners were in there mopping up a leak; much to the embarrassment of the organisers! Drug use is just a part of modern society which will never be stopped. There has never been a drugs-related death on a scooter rally, and there are more people who over-indulge dangerously with alcohol than Class A drugs.

As the Sunday afternoon pub crawl begins, usually soaking up the sunshine outside the Crown at the top of Union Street, we gather waifs and strays along the way as we sample every bar we pass, until our merry band of friends and acquaintances fills each pub we go in. It's hard to explain the Sunday Club atmosphere, but it's always a good laugh; we're in fine spirits

By the time most hardened Sunday Club drinkers arrive at the Balcony Club, this is how the world looks.

days, cocaine, ecstasy and cannabis are the most commonly used narcotics. Three or four hard days away, with very little sleep, and the average age of Scooterists reaching over 40, mean it's hard for many to keep going without at least some form of chemical assistance!

The use of drugs, especially the 'love drug' ecstasy, a few years ago helped people to overcome the anger which caused trouble during the 1980s and '90s. Ecstasy helped to forge bonds between people who wouldn't even have sat in the same pub as one and other, let alone spend a full weekend socialising! For all the damage that drugs do, recreational drug use has also solved a lot of social problems, and chilled people out. As long as the people involved in their use behave responsibly, as most do, and are careful with where and when they use them, the general public has no reason to be alarmed or worried. The regular front page *News of the World* headlines 'Soap star in cocaine-fuelled bender' is sensationalism at its worst. Every club, pub and party

Silliness is the order of the day; daft hats are the norm!

and make our own entertainment as we drink our way through town. With fewer people in town it's much easier to get served at the bar, and you can bond with people you don't usually get the time to speak to. Try it one bank holiday Sunday, but don't tell everybody or you'll spoil things for the rest of us!

By the time the Sunday Club arrives at the do in the Balcony Club above the bowling alley, we'll have been drinking for around eleven hours, non-stop, and, although the venue is much quieter than the ice stadium, you can still expect to see 700 people in there, and it soon livens up.

Elsewhere in town other promoters are holding their own wrap parties, and the last records of the weekend end in cheers from the appreciative audience.

Monday morning, and it's time for the die hards to pack up their tents and head for home. Another fantastic Isle of Wight scooter rally is over, unless you're one of the organisers and have to pick up litter on the campsite after the 3000 campers have left! In the case of most of the VFM crew and a couple of hundred friends there's still another night to go before they head for home on Tuesday morning.

Many Scooterists treat the end of August as their summer holiday and continue riding along the south coast of Britain, stopping at various seaside towns along the way, before ending up at the Mersea Island rally in Essex.

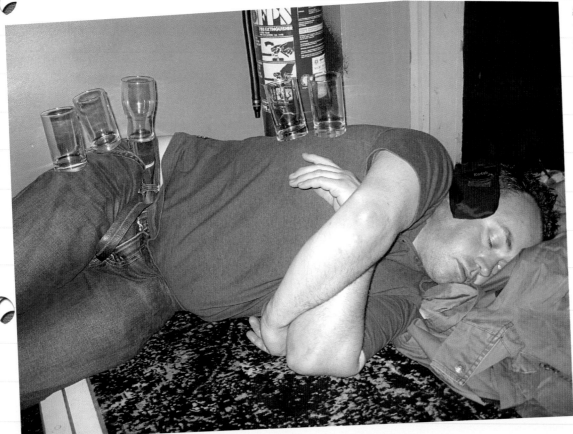

The day can take its toll. A great advert warning against the perils of binge drinking!

6

Daytrippers

Although so far we've concentrated on the rally-going Scooterist, there's another, parallel, scene which is just as big as the national rallies but is more regionally-based. It's made up (mainly) of scooter riders who don't feel the need to ride hundreds of miles for a weekend away at the seaside, but they still love riding scooters and meeting up with like-minded souls.

The scooter alliances were set up to bring individual Scooterists and clubs in each area together, which in turn helps the attendance at regional club events. Yorkshire, Lancashire and the East Midlands are three of the most well known and largest alliances.

Jeff Johnson, secretary for the East Midlands Scooter Alliance, gave us an insight into what his alliance sets out to achieve:

"The Scooter, scene since its inception, has always been evolving, and alliances have come into their own as part of that evolution process, mainly due to the fact that we now live in a 24/7 society. For

Jeff Johnno mans the EMSA stall at Beat the Bikers 2007.

The meeting point for EMSA runs soon fills up!

many, long gone are the days of striving to finish work early on a Friday, so you could ride to a rally with your club or mates en mass.

"People have more disposable income than ever before, but the downside to that is family. Many alliance members are scooter enthusiasts from the past who rode scooters since leaving school. Then, as they grew older, they found they had to cut back due to having a family, the inevitable mortgage, and the wife's desire for the family package holiday. The extra income required to bring up a family and still enjoy your hobby to the full means partners may have to work weekends, which is the one part of the week that major scooter events take place. As a consequence, rally numbers dropped, and this can be seen (in my opinion) at Great Yarmouth more than anywhere else. Bank holiday rally numbers also suffer due to

Whether or not you like Mod-style scooters, you can't argue that this TV175 is as cool as anything on the road.

Roads quickly fill up with over 500 scooters; not bad for a Sunday ride out!

The spectacle of hundreds of scooters riding together is one of the best ways of attracting newcomers, and old riders back on to two wheels.

people leaving the rally on a Sunday because they have to work on the Monday, or in some cases all the holiday weekend.

"Alliances have filled this void by organising events that take place largely on Sundays, thus avoiding the need to stay out all weekend. This not only pleases the wife financially, but only takes

Egg runs like this EMSA-organised Mansfield event are a great way to introduce kids to scooter riding; they love it!

for members (which is proving difficult). When organised properly, alliances can provide local scooter enthusiasts with many benefits the solo or club riders alone cannot achieve.

"EMSA is run on an optional member's scheme basis, which sets us apart from other organisations. Basically, that means anyone can come along and join in the events, but only by becoming an official member do you receive the best benefits.

Matlock is usually the preserve of bikers on a Sunday, but not when EMSA is in town!

This Yorkshire Alliance run coincided with the Scarborough scooter rally, and brought the seaside town to a complete standstill.

a few hours out of the weekend too. The East Midland Scooter Alliance was started by Andy Quail and myself with the idea of organising ride outs to club events/ fun days and our own destinations, like Matlock Bath, where entire clubs and solo riders can all ride together in numbers up to and above the 500 mark. Scooter club charity events benefit from the larger numbers turning up at Easter egg runs, toy runs, or local charitable events and, as a large organisation, we have been able to negotiate discounts at local scooter shops throughout the East Midlands region, to the benefit of our members. I'm currently working on insurance companies to provide cheaper insurance

This adds great credibility to EMSA as we are an officially recognised body. Once companies see that we work on a professional level, they are more willing to back us on that premise. Good, organised alliances should be able to provide a bridge from the national scene to the local scene without one

their TV200 or Vespa GS for a packet of fags and a pint way back in the 1960s, '70s and '80s, have got back into the scene as a direct result of seeing the alliance ride outs in a town near to their home. The spark of nostalgia is easily re-ignited after watching up to seven hundred brightly coloured, noisy scooters passing by in a cloud of blue smoke, or having had a quiet family picnic taken over as one of

The term 'born again' is often used to describe older riders reliving their youth.

Scooterists meet up in various local towns on the morning of an alliance run.

detracting from the other; uniting clubs and solo riders, whilst catering for the needs of both. Scootering is no longer a young person's hobby, it's a lifestyle that gets into your blood. And just because you have a family should not mean you cannot incorporate what you love into your life; and alliances do this unequivocally.

"EMSA is run by a committee consisting of a chairman, secretary and a minimum of six people; it has its own constitution and is charitable registered."

To give you an idea of how big the alliances have become, the Yorkshire Alliance boasts a membership of over 80 Yorkshire-based scooter clubs, not to mention the individual members! The north of England has always been a scootering stronghold, from Leicester to Nottingham and Leeds to Manchester there has always been quite a healthy scene, and over the past few years it's grown and grown.

Many scooter riders who hung up their battered piss pot helmets and swapped

Getting into scooters again forty years after you sold your last one is much more fun than owning an allotment!

the alliance ride outs visits a local beauty spot on a Sunday afternoon!

These older scooter riders have money to burn, and will happily pay any price to get a second chance to relive their youth.

They soon started snapping up all the half-decent secondhand scooters, and eBay became the source of many rusty restoration projects. Scooter prices quickly started to rise and, before anybody realised what was happening, the cost of vintage Lambrettas and classic Vespas rose astronomically, meaning the average, younger, Scooterist struggled to get on the road on their preferred model and had to settle for a less popular machine instead. Scooters which at one time would hardly get a second glance, like the Lambretta LDs and even Starstream, were suddenly worth a fortune – or they were to the desperados who were prepared to fork out their life savings for anything with a Lambretta badge on its battered and rusting legshields. Value can only be determined by what somebody is willing to pay.

A typical 'born again' Scooterist will be male and in his late forties or early fifties. He'll ride a restored SX 200, Li125, Vespa GS 160, or a modern scooter like a Vespa PX. His scooter will usually (but not always) be adorned with original and hard to find embellishments, as well as the stereotypical lights, mirrors and racks. The rider will dress in a similar fashion to the way he dressed as a twenty year old. He'll quite often wear a parka, covered in patches, the obligatory targets, Union Jacks and 'Mod' badges are favourites, and he'll ride in an open faced helmet.

Since the

Lights and mirrors are more popular now than they ever have been.

A TV175 in this condition could make £7000 at auction.

rise of the so called 'born again Scooterist' (a phenomenon argued over and debated about in many a magazine letter and bar room), the sales of lights, mirrors, crash bars and chrome accessories has quadrupled, and the price of a restored Lambretta has gone through the roof. A pristine example of a sought after Lambretta TV175 can fetch £7000 at an internet auction, but the born again Scooterists have plenty of disposable income since paying off their mortgages, and they relish the thought of telling their new found

The useless parts in this box were removed from a 'restored' Vietnamese scooter; be careful what you buy!

SCOOTER LIFESTYLE

Providing the alliance events aren't on at the same time as a national rally, you'll see plenty of rally-going Scooterists there as well.

friends on internet forums just how much they paid for their nut and bolt Taiwanese restoration job, complete with whip aerial and fog horns!

The current crop of Taiwanese scooters look great on the internet auction sites where they're usually sold and, when they arrive in their crates, the average owner will be chuffed to bits, to begin with at least. I can't claim that all Vietnamese scooters being shipped to the UK are dangerous or not quite as advertised, but there are plenty of bad ones being sold to unsuspecting punters. I've been called out to shops by disbelieving owners, to look at Vietnamese scooters with a wide range of alarming and often quite dangerous problems. Engine shims made from tin cans, broken engine parts bodged and installed, whitewall tyres with internal cracks, frames welded together – you name it and the resourceful Vietnamese mechanics can bodge it. When you live in a country where parts and money are hard to come by you adapt and mend rather than buy new. These skills have been passed down through generations of ardent bodgers, and the restored and pristine-looking scooters being sold to unsuspecting British Scooterists may not always be quite as good as they seem.

The prices of these machines may look like a bargain, and providing you or a competent scooter mechanic are prepared to look over the scooter thoroughly once you receive it you'll not go far wrong. Be sure to get the engine, brakes, hubs, wheel rims, tyres, shock absorber and forks thoroughly checked over for your own piece of mind and safety.

It's also worth checking that the model is as the advert claims. There have been a number of scooters which actually share the same duplicated frame number, and the stamps can look less than genuine. Buying a Vietnamese scooter may be a cheap way to get the model of your dreams (or something that looks close to it at a distance) but the unwary could find it turns into a nightmare!

Not all scooter riders who organise and attend the various alliance ride outs are 'born agains', though; there are also plenty of well-established clubs and riders who enjoy the camaraderie and

buzz created by seeing so many scooters in their local area. Rally going Scooterists play quite a large part in this scene, and will attend most local alliance events, providing they don't clash with another national rally.

Club marshals often lead the procession, and stop traffic at junctions and traffic lights.

From March to October one of the regional alliances will hold a Sunday ride out almost every week and, as well as Scooterists from the area, they will often attract scooter riders from other parts of the country who will travel for a few hours to take part in the mass ride out.

"The meeting place will often be at a large pub or well-known landmark, and the riders will bring traffic to a standstill as they make their way noisily to their destination, where there will be some form of entertainment laid on, including a bouncy castle for the kids, and a few trade stalls, and maybe a disco or band.

Occasionally a police escort will accompany the procession, stopping cars at junctions and allowing the riders to go through red traffic lights. If the police aren't able to attend, alliance volunteers will don fluorescent vests and act as marshals to try and get the riders safely to their destination and keep the massive group together, which is much easier said than done!

There's no mistaking that the alliance ride outs have helped to breathe some new life into the scooter scene as a whole, and boosted the profits of scooter dealers from around the world, many of whom have benefited from the increase in prices and also managed to shift loads of old tat that had been gathering dust at the back of the store room since the *Quadrophenia* revival waned.

As well as ride outs, most of the alliances also put on weekend rallies of their own, and they're always well-supported by friends and alliance members, as well as attracting Scooterists from further afield.

The so called 'born again' Scooterists who are usually middle-aged, are often ridiculed for their style of dress and the way their scooters are customised, they're also (quite rightly) blamed for the massive hike in scooter prices by the die hard Scooterists, who have stuck with the scene through good times and bad. Whether you like the older generation coming back into the scene or not, there's no mistaking the fact that they have helped to nurture the local scooter scene. Many new clubs have sprung up as a direct result of the Sunday ride outs, and at least a few members of these clubs have started attending the national scooter rallies once their eyes have been opened to its existence.

Love them or loathe them they're a part of our diverse culture and, as far as I'm concerned, any publicity for the scootering way of life is worth

The Alliances have helped the local scooter scene, and the national rallies have also benefited as a result. Youngsters are finally starting to ride scooters again.

having. If it helps to protect our scene for future generations (and us in our old age) then it can only be a positive way forward. I may not be ready to buy a parka just yet, but who knows what I'll be doing in another twenty years' time ...

The thing that helps the scooter scene stay alive is the rich variety of people and diverse cultures that come together, united by a common bond.

7 Scooter racing and tuning

If you talk about scooters to the average non-rider, their immediate impression of a scooter is the stereotypical 'hairdryer' with small wheels, dodgy handling and low capacity vintage engines. It all adds up to what should be a scooter that would be ideal for a Granny to do her shopping on.

After the war people needed some cheap and practical transport to rebuild the ravaged countries of Europe. Man likes to tinker, though, and, if it's got wheels and an engine, there's always a way to make it go faster.

During the 1960s a club scene developed, and most clubs at the time didn't welcome the 'troublesome' Mods who had been making the headlines after their bank holiday seaside clashes. Instead, enthusiasts came together and held weekend events, which would usually consist of a social get-together and a few reliability trials or gymkhanas (where the riders would tackle obstacles on their scooters) and, occasionally, there'd be road racing. Piaggio and Innocenti both fielded factory teams in a bid to prove their supremacy. Most of the riders would ride there on their scooters, compete on them and ride the same machine home again afterwards; they simply didn't have the spare cash to own more than one scooter (or a van) to get to meetings.

The Isle of Man was one of the favourite destinations, with the annual scooter week being a popular event on the calendar. If you speak to any long serving scooter rider who was active in the 1960s and 1970s you'll soon be shown photos of the person in question splashing through the ford at Druidale on the island during a time trial, and you'll

Scooter trials and gymkhanas like this one have virtually died out. The 2001 foot and mouth outbreak stopped events like these and grass tracking for a while and they've never recovered.

Twisty sprints and hill climbs were another popular part of racing up until the early nineties; they've virtually disappeared now, though.

also be shown the competitor's treasured medals and trophies. These events were the predecessors of modern scooter racing, and during the 1970s circuit racing became popular.

Up until the 1990s, scooter racing had always been able to stand on its own two feet (or wheels as the case may be) but, as the social scene began to decline, attendance at all scooter related events suffered as a result. The cost of race entries began to rise and, before long, drastic action was necessary to secure the long term survival of the sport.

A typical race meeting in the 1990s would be held at such tracks as the tight and twisty Three Sisters kart track in Wigan, Pembrey in south Wales,

beautiful Cadwell Park in Lincolnshire, or flat and featureless Snetterton in Norfolk.

The 'Standards' was one of the most popular classes, made up of 150cc and 200cc full-framed Lambrettas, and a good selection of gorgeous Vespa 90SSs. The 'Specials', or group six as it was known, was the equivalent to the MotoGP class ... well, sort of.

A group six machine was usually a highly-tuned Lambretta with all of the non-essential parts removed. Fuel would be carried inside the tubular steel frame, rather than in a separate fuel tank, to save weight, motorcycle style rear sets would be fitted to keep the rider in an aerodynamic crouch,

Above: A typical scooter racing grid, circa 1990 at Cadwell.

Below: The paddock has always been a friendly place in scooter racing; teams will often swap parts ... unless, of course, they're a class rival!

Ralph Saxelby's modern group six machine looks gorgeous naked, and has taken years of development to perfect.

A young Mark Broadhurst with Graham Gee's Team MB group six bike, 1990.

as the frame and engine were originally fitted to the scooter. The engines were tuned to 240cc or 250cc and, sometimes, even water cooled. Many tuning parts and accessories which road going Scooterists take for granted (like cylinder kits, exhausts, clutches, ignitions, shock absorbers and disc brakes) started life being developed on the race track, before eventually being adapted for use in road going scooters.

The rallies weren't the only part of scootering to suffer dramatically during the 1990s. Race meetings also had a sharp and noticeable decline, and the NSRA decided to take over the running of race events from the well established FBSC (Federation of British Scooter Clubs). The BSSO or British Scooter Sport Organisation was born, but it wasn't popular with everybody. Many of the old timers resented the take-over and dropped out of racing completely, but the move appealed to some of the younger Scooterists who had been involved with the rally scene and thought the new regime would breathe a bit of new life into the old organisation.

The drop in the number of race entrants, and stricter insurance restrictions at tracks meant it was no longer financially viable for the BSSO to hire race circuits for scooter only meetings, so it started to share meetings with motorcycle racing clubs.

The new style meetings have been run in this way ever since, and there's a hard core of regular

and bike-style fairings became popular additions to help achieve the perfect way for the machine to slice through the air and increase top speed. Virtually anything was allowed in group six, as long

The grid at Three Sisters in 2007 represents a good cross section of scootering; although it's not visible, the small frame Vespa is starting to make a comeback as well.

racers who compete for the BSSO championship each season. The various scooter racing groups form on the grid at the same time to ensure a decent race for both riders and spectators alike, and the results are split into different classes at the end of the race.

In recent times the most popular classes are the 200cc standards, which are entirely made up of Lambrettas, and they provide some fast and very close racing. Another popular class is the 70cc autos; the class is dominated by lightweight Piaggio Zips. Although a few people have tried racing other models of scooter, the Aprilia SR, for instance, and most recently the Derbi GP-1. The Zips are fast, light, and very agile, and they often prove a match for some of the larger capacity geared scooters, and there's plenty of argy bargy and fairing bashing on track.

One or two well known bike racers started their early careers on Piaggio Zips, including Leon Haslam who won the Piaggio Zip championship at the age of just 13, and World Superbike star James Toseland,

so it's quite a good way to start a career in racing, and kids as young as 11 can take part.

The Specials, or group six as it was known, have made a bit of a comeback recently with RS Tunings' Ralph Saxelby proving who the boss is on his beautiful, pastel green cut down and very fast Lambretta, a machine which he's been developing and perfecting for the past twenty years. There are also one or two modern autos being used to good effect in the Specials class. Eddie Goode is a regular on his chopped about Gilera Runner, although a nasty accident at Lydden in September 2007 left him out for the rest of the season. Current 125cc British bike championship rider, Scott Rodgers, obliterated the competition in 2005 on the Ryan Saxelby-tuned, PSN Scooters, Italjet Dragster. Scott provided some thrilling no-holds-barred racing, and his talent has been missed on track since he moved back to bike racing in 2006.

The scooter sidecars are often neglected by the organising clubs, officials, and fellow racers, as are bike racing sidecars but, nevertheless, the

The racing is fast and furious, with plenty of knee-down action on track. James Campen leads on his stunning yellow Lammy.

Charlie Edmonds won the BSSO championship in 2006 and 2007.

three-wheeled outfits still provide some good racing. Despite the sidecars often being left till the final race of the day, and more often than not missing their second race due to failing light or an incident hit meeting over-running its time slot, the regular sidecar teams still turn up at every meeting.

Ralph Remnant and passenger, PJ McLavery have been the masters of three-wheeled action for the past few years, and the dazzling duo has dominated the sport on the distinctive orange Lambretta outfit. The auto engines have slowly started to make an impact on the sidecar class in recent times. One of the fastest auto outfits is owned

by Danny Millard and his passenger, Kathryn Renwick. The mean, black, 172cc Piaggio-engined machine has started to prove a match for Ralph

Three of the top riders battle for supremacy at Three Sisters. Charlie Edmonds leads Stuart Day, whilst Jon Ulndell tries to ride around the outside.

On the track, the RS Tuning machine is a force to be reckoned with.

Ralph Remnant and PJ Mclaverty are the undisputed kings of three-wheeled scooter racing.

Remnant, but it will take a good few years before they can even dream of matching Ralph's eleven championship wins! Sadly for scooter sport, Ralph and PJ have semi-retired and are currently trying their hand at racing a 600cc Honda outfit, but they still bring their Lambretta out at some of their favourite tracks.

Racing suffered another decline in 2006 but, after a revamp, which included some new circuits being introduced and a couple of old favourites being put back on the calendar, as well as a modern approach to racing and some higher profile advertising (which includes a new forum) and website (check out www.scooterracing.org.uk for more information). The sport has made a good recovery and seems to be on the rise again.

By the end of the 2007 season the grids were full, and, at the final round in October there was even a reserve list. Newcomers during the season

included a pair of eleven-year-old lads. Matthew and Kurt Wigley, fresh from mini motos (they should be household names in a few years). The brothers used scooter racing as a stepping stone to gain enough signatures on their race licences to enable them to fast track their way into bike racing at an earlier age than the competition.

Apart from track-based scooter racing, there's also a popular scooter sprint scene which is held on ¼ mile drag strips (Elvington and Santa Pod are two of the regular tracks) and the fastest riders at the moment are Joe Elliot on the PM Tuning auto sprinter, and Stuart Owen on his '100mph Lambretta'.

Sprinting is popular with many of the auto riders who benefit from the increased reliability and relatively easy tuning of their modern scooters. A highly-tuned auto is capable of producing over 36bhp and can still be used as a road going scooter, providing the owner is willing to keep on top of

Stuart Owen prepares to obliterate the competition on the dyno at Run to the Shires with his www.100-mph-lambretta.com sprinter. He recorded a terminal dyno speed of 124mph!

indeed had any desire to, almost all of them will have benefited from its existence simply because of the tuning goodies developed on tracks over the years.

Scooter tuning is big business, and the majority of road going Scooterists will have at least some form of engine modification to enhance performance, or arguably decrease reliability! Malossi, Polini, TS1, Mugello and Imola kits are must have bolt-ons for many scooter riders. Vespa owners favour the Malossi or Polini kits, which can produce good results when fitted properly and when the casings have been matched to suit. For many years Lambretta owners have stuck with the tried and tested TS1 kit. Other kits have come and gone, the Honda 205 for instance, but the TS1 has always been the 'Daddy'.

All good things come to an end, though, and recent development has seen a new Lambretta kit hitting the road. AF Rayspeed has been developing a new road going kit for the Lambretta. Launched in summer 2007, the RB22 is a welcome and eagerly anticipated addition. Early results have proved more than favourable and, although there have been a few teething problems during the first year of production, it looks like the RB kit (which consists of a head, barrel and piston) will be a success. It's quite an impressive-looking piece of aluminium art, and will provide the focus of animated chatter at dinner parties if passed around the dining table between courses!

The RB22 gives a good spread of power and is easily capable of producing a whopping 26bhp when set up correctly; using the right blend of ingredients, including the all important exhaust which has been specially developed to suit the new kit. You'll also need a beefy crank, well set-up carb, correct gear ratios, and casings ported to suit.

The RB feels very smooth through the gears, with no noticeable drop in power between third and fourth, unlike many tuned scooters, and the 250cc RB kit is likely to be even better.

The TS1 has, perhaps, after over twenty years of service, had its day, but it'll still be around for a good few years to come. The TS1 boys who have grown up with Terry Shepherd's popular kit will undoubtedly keep replacing their worn out barrels with yet another TS1, rather than trying the new kid on the block, but eventually the RB22 kit will take over where the TS1 left off.

regular maintenance. The latest progression of the auto sprinter is PM Tuning's twin cylinder machine which will, undoubtedly, be the first of many high-powered twin autos in the future.

One thing is for sure, no matter what happens, there will always be scooter racing in one form or another. It might not attract large name sponsors, there's little or no television coverage, and race winners are lucky if they even get a plastic trophy, but scooter sport is still friendly, relatively cheap to have a go at, and its great fun to watch, and even better to compete in; give it a go ...

Although many active scooter riders have probably never visited a scooter race meeting, or

My own Malossi 210-equipped, Ryan Saxelby-tuned Vespa PX200 disc. 19.9bhp and 94mph on the dyno.

The RB22 kit, complete with exhaust, carb, crank, and reed block.

Check out the ports on this RB22 barrel. It's been known for small animals to be fished out of the inlet!

The custom scene

Ever since scooters started being embraced by trendsetting youngsters during the 1960s, the machines have been customised in one way or another, whether it be bolt-on accessories, a chrome front rack and crash bars, for example, or maybe even the odd mirror or two. The 'Mod style' scooter, or 'Christmas tree' as they're affectionately known by the average Scooterist, is just the tip of the proverbial customising iceberg.

Every outsider's idea of a custom scooter looks just like this. Each to their own, of course, but there are plenty of other things to do to our humble machines.

The trend for customising scooters is as popular now (if not more so) as it was during the *Quadrophenia* revival of the late-seventies and early-eighties. As with any kind of style, trends come and go on a regular basis, and a custom scooter can range from a standard-looking Vespa PX125 with a few bolt-on goodies, to a cut down and well engineered Lambretta, or a full-blown, custom-painted and airbrushed show-winning masterpiece.

Customising is all about expressing the owner's individuality. Some owners have the ability to carry out most of the work themselves, which keeps costs to a minimum, but the usual route is to 'farm out' most stages of the project to various custom specialists.

There are plenty of well-established airbrush artists around the country; John Spurgeon of Norwich-based Aerographics is, literally, a living

Street racers suit scooters perfectly. This Vespa Rally may be thirty-years-old, but, with its paintwork and trick tuning parts, it looks as modern as anything out there.

Choppers are back in fashion; check out the artwork on this tank.

legend who has sprayed many of the top show-winning custom scooters over the last twenty odd years. Another notable artist is Dave Dickinson of Bridlington. Dave has been producing some classic scooters recently, including the show-winning scoots, Fairground Attraction and Harbour Lights.

A custom scooter builder will employ the talents of a number of different specialists during the course of a project. Engraving is one of the tasks usually only entrusted to a small number of artists, Don Blocksidge and Pete Robinson being two of the most sought after metal inscribers in the country. Chrome and gold plating also need to be done properly, the most widely used firms are Karl Russell's Quality Chrome in Hull, and Trev Harrison at Midas Touch in Leeds. The London Chroming Company also gets good feedback from custom owners, and it's worth using tried and tested scooter specialists (recommended by others) wherever possible, rather than some local, back street industrial chrome plater who usually coats bits of machinery rather than concourse winning scooters. Cost cutting can prove costly in the long run!

Many custom owners find a theme which interests them. The owner of this fantastic PX, Nick Pegg, has used some of his life experiences to customise his scooter.

Some of the well-known chrome platers will offer scooter parts 'off the shelf' in exchange for your old parts. This can significantly cut down on the time you're left waiting for your shiny parts to arrive, building custom scooters is something that really will try the patience of the builder, and it's not uncommon for an owner to wait a year or two for his paintwork to be finished if using one of the top artists!

Customising can take many forms, and can be as cheap or expensive as you like, especially these days with modern computer-aided design and vinyl graphics companies who can take a piece of artwork and apply it to your side panel while you wait. The

Paul Pinder's show winning Fairground Attraction, was sprayed by Dave Dickinson.

Engraving may not be to everybody's taste, but there's no denying it looks sensational when done properly.

finished result won't look quite as good as an original airbrushed artwork, when examined closely anyway, but the cost saving and instant results take some beating. Vinyl graphics are perfect for street racer type scooters, or where the owner wants lots of lettering as part of the design. A full-framed vinyl-wrapped

When it comes to chrome, Karl Russell is one of the best known names on the scooter circuit. Here's a subtle little Vespa he's recently built.

This Spiderman-themed Lambretta uses the latest vinyl wrapping technique; £500 job done!

scooter can be done for as little as £500, and will be produced very quickly. The current specialist in this field is Custom Scooter Art in Doncaster, but I'm sure there'll soon be plenty of firms offering a similar service.

Nut and bolt restoration jobs may not be regarded as customising by many, but to turn a battered and rusty vintage scooter into a machine which looks as good, if not better than when it first rolled off Innocenti's Italian production line in 1959 is hard to achieve. Restoration of vintage scooters has always been quite big business, and a handful of

dealers cater exclusively for this growing market. As a result, there are dozens of show-winning, standard-looking vintage Lambrettas and Vespas which enter custom shows around the UK and Europe.

Many Scooterists find the idea of restoring a scooter back to standard spec a waste of time and prefer to create something a little more imaginative instead ...

As the average age of the active Scooterist increases so does the need for reliability, and modern, automatic scooters have provided the

This lovely Li looks like it's just rolled off the production line.

Subtle restoration can be as good as a full custom job when it's done properly, like on this Series 2 Lammy.

Lee Edmonds from Swadlincote built and sprayed this unusual Lammy street racer, fitted with an auto engine.

Another well-built Lammy, pictured at Bridlington.

Street racers have been popular for the past twenty years, and still work well on a Vespa or Lambretta.

At first glance you may think this Lambretta LD is just another tidy restoration. Look a bit closer, though, and you'll discover it's been fitted with a modern auto engine by Dave Briggs of Grimsby.

To look at from the front this could be just an ordinary, tidy Lambretta, but it's actually a Series 5 auto conversion by Frank Sanderson.

ideal compromise of speed and ease of use. It's pretty common to find Lambrettas (and occasionally Vespas) fitted with the engine from an Italjet Dragster or Gilera Runner. The actual engine transplant isn't quite as straightforward as you may think, though, and it takes a fair amount of cutting and welding to get the engine and frame to mate perfectly, not to mention sorting out the electrics and water cooling system. Although the DIY route is possible (providing the builder has the necessary skills to carry out the conversion safely) the most common route is to use a firm which specialises in frame/engine conversions.

Frank Sanderson of Lambretta Innovations in Preston has been involved with this type of work for over twenty years. In the early days Frank was partly responsible for creating the original Rosser 350. The Rossers sprang up in the late 1980s, and utilised a powerful Yamaha YPVS 350 engine mated to a Lambretta frame. The man behind the Rosser had great ideas but, sadly, his business sense wasn't exactly admirable, and he ripped off a number of Scooterists before disappearing. Years later, karma caught up with Alan Rosser, though, and a bullet finished him off – live by the sword, die by the sword; or gun, as the case may be ...

Frank Sanderson is well known these days for his Lambretta auto engine conversions, and he also dabbles in bike engine conversions. The Series 4 and

for close friends and associates, and many of his creations have featured in the pages of *Scootering* magazine, and even the occasional bike magazine.

Recent 'Insane' creations include the stunning 'Two Worlds Collide' auto-engined Lambretta Series 2, and a very trick auto-engined Vespa with lift up bodywork called 'Nero 'o Paco' which translates as 'matt black'! Ferdy has also built his own radical matt black chopper which features a foot-operated clutch and 'suicide shift' hand gear change. One thing is for sure, Ferdy always has something new up his sleeve, and there will be plenty more Insane Innovations scooters

Ferdy, of Insane Innovations, works on the snake-like exhaust for his chopper.

Series 5 Lambrettas created by Frank are a common sight at rallies, and Frank has developed a number of specialist parts which the DIY builder can use to speed up the process of building an auto Lammy at home. His parts include complete frame kits, which are ready for the engine to bolt straight in to, and twin disc brake conversions fitted to Lambretta widened forks, as well as widened fibreglass Lambretta panels which are necessary to hide the extra width of the Piaggio auto engines.

Ferdy built this scooter for himself, aptly titled Insane! Check out the rear end, made from part of a Lambretta fork and mono shock.

Another well-respected specials builder is Ferdy of Insane Innovations in Leicestershire. Ferdy only builds scooters as a hobby, but his limitless imagination, skill, and use of a welder and angle grinder are second to none. Ferdy builds scooters in the custom-built shed at the bottom of his garden where these ones came from. If you ever wondered why he's called 'Insane Innovations' here's what he came up with during a ten minute chat in his shed. Ideas spout from Ferdy like a gushing geyser and he hardly comes up for breath between ideas. It's hard to keep up with him as his thoughts and

as well. I'll make it rigid with a sprung seat mounted low down just off the back wheel, maybe pivoted off a mountain bike shock.

"If I had a tube bender I'd be laughing, I've got an idea for a frame that you probably wouldn't be able to ride but it'd look shit hot. Why not build one that looks really stupid? I thought of something on the way to the tip today. You have the back wheel further up towards the front and another wheel behind it to keep the wheelbase right, so they're both still

Two Worlds Collide, an Insane Series 2 Lambretta with 172cc Piaggio auto engine. Simply stunning.

ideas are regurgitated before you have time to process the information ...

"I'm just going to use scooter panels and make a complete frame, make it a bit longer than a Lammy so I can get 13 inch wheels in and get good tyres. I'm thinking about putting one of those Kwak engines in. It's a 650 water cooled Verysys. They're fairly new, I'm thinking why not build something that you can get bits for in a few years? If I do everything a couple of inches bigger than a Lammy, everything will be in scale. I'm not sure about the gearing, though, so I'll have the sprocket on another little counter shaft so I can change the gearing on that.

"I'm doing a Rod model Vespa auto as well; I'll make a new subframe so you can take it off using six bolts. Good solid engineering, but basic stuff, you can't go wrong. I want to do a few different types of scooter, then I've got a range. I can do Lammy autos, I can do Vespas, do a chop. I want to do another chop

This Insane chopper is a work of art. You really need to study it to appreciate the work Ferdy put into creating it.

driving but I don't know how it'd corner. It'd look like something out of Thunderbirds!

"Another idea was to have another engine on top of the original one with the two wheels rubbing against each other, would it drive the other one? It's got to work, though. Or maybe a friction drive crosser engine ..."

Ferdy certainly has the talent, foresight, dedication and enough ground-breaking innovative ideas to keep him busy in the Insane Innovations shed for the next few years at least.

Ferdy's chopper is just one of many fantastic

'Sacrilege' an extra wide Vespa with moulded and frenched bodywork.

creations to hit our roads recently. The influence of television programmes like *American Chopper* and *Biker Build Off* have kick-started chopper building once again. Matt black chops often look like they've been literally thrown together and, in some cases, it's only the coat of paint holding them in one piece, but many

These two Lammy choppers take design cues from the bike world; perfectly executed and every bit as well put together as anything the Americans can build.

of them are as well thought out and cleverly built and engineered as anything you'll see on TV. In fact, one of the well-known faces from *Biker Build Off*, Russ Mitchell of Exile Cycles, was a Scooter Boy back in the 1980s, and his Lambretta chopper, Exile, which was featured in *Scootering* many years ago, is still talked about today.

Scooterists often take ideas and inspiration from the bike world, and the age old 'Mods and Rockers' rivalry has died down to nothing more than harmless banter and hazy

This pearl white stunner was pictured at VFM's scooter-only event in Buxton in 2007.

Mick Gauntlett's 'Steve', a strange name for a scooter, but who needs a name anyway?

recollections over the years. Although there are still people from both factions who show animosity to their 'rivals', most bike and scooter riders have mutual respect for each other. To prove a point, a *Quadrophenia*-themed custom Lambretta even won the best of show trophy at the National Chopper Club's annual Rock & Blues custom show in 2007, an event attended by 15,000 hardened bikers! A few years ago the Lambretta would have been sacrificed over a camp fire at a bike rally, and the thought of one winning a show would have caused nightmares for the organisers.

Custom projects can be as expensive or as cheap as you like. It's not unknown for a project to cost over £20,000, but as long as the owner puts his heart and soul into creating a scooter which reflects his or her own tastes, interests, and thoughts, it doesn't matter whether it wins trophies or not; it's all about having a sense of style and creating the machine of your dreams.

9

I am one of the faces!

I'm sure most people reading this book will have seen the classic Mod film, *Quadrophenia*. If you have, you'll no doubt remember Jimmy uttering the immortal words, "I am one of the faces." A 'face' is somebody who is well known on the scene. They'll often be involved with the organisation and running of events, for example, or may be the face behind a large scooter-based business, but many of them will just be ordinary Scooterists, admired and respected for what they bring to the rallies. Someone can be a 'face' because of a flamboyant dress sense, beautiful or unusual custom scooter, uncanny sense of humour, long history with scooters, lively attitude, or just for the fact that they seem to be everywhere you go.

There are literally hundreds of faces who should be immortalised, or at least recognised but, sadly, there's not enough space for everybody in this book. The faces are as important to the scene as the scooters themselves, and, for many rally goers, it's being part of that clique which appeals to them. Most faces travel thousands of miles by scooter every year to attend events (or to put them on) and, come rain or shine, they'll be propping up the bar at a rally destination somewhere every single weekend. Whether it's a national event, a local club do, or a foreign rally you'll see them there.

Many of these faces don't get the recognition they deserve, and, although they're well known for what they do or how they look, it's not often people get the chance to see what makes them tick.

To provide a snapshot, and to show the diversity of scooter enthusiasts, we caught up with three very different people to see what brought them to the scooter scene, and, more importantly, what keeps them there after all these years.

Norrie Kerr

One name any self-respecting Scooterist will know, particularly if you stand on the Vespa side of the fence, is Mr Norrie Kerr. Norrie may not be a regular rally-going Scooterist, but his involvement behind the scenes has kept scooter riders and racers on the road and track for years.

Norrie is probably best known for being one half of Midland Scooter Centre, up until 1990; he's also well known for his small frame Vespa tuning and racing.

These days the likeable

Norrie Kerr puts his Vespa 90SS through its paces at Baitings Dam.

Scot runs well known importer VE UK, a trade supplier for scooter and bike parts and accessories, including its best known line Malossi. Norrie is also President of the British Scooter Sporting Organisation, and has a long standing history with scooters, Scooterists, and the famous Italian steed, Vespa.

Norrie managed to spare an hour or two from his busy schedule to let us know a bit about himself, and how his life-long love affair with scooters began.

How did you first get involved with scooters? "I went to Canada for three years, married my wife there and brought her home two days later, which made me hugely popular with her family, as you can imagine. I had my first bike that year, 1966. I had a Vespa because it was the first scooter I came across; it could have been a Lambretta, I suppose, but I had the wee Vespa. I was working as a clippie on the trolley buses and had to be on the 5.15am bus, and had to carry my tin with the machine in it and a bag, and they'd fit on the Vespa floorboards. The scooter never used to start, though; I had to bump it every morning down the hill. The wife used to stand at the window waving to make sure I got away.

"I met a guy, who lived across the road, Richard, who went on to become a roadie for Hawkwind. Richard had a Lambretta series 2, and I had a Sportique. We were down in Dunoon on the Clyde coast once when Richard said, "What's this lot coming down here on scooters?" Some of them had leather jackets on and Barbour suits, we had parkas on and all the business. Richard saw them and said, "Where the fuck's all this lot going?" They pulled up and it turned out they were the Glasgow Vespa Club, and one of them only lived a couple of streets away from me in Govern Hill, although we'd never met. I went down the club on the Tuesday and that was it, I was there for ever.

"Being a Scot and part of the club meant we had this thing where we like to travel to England and stick it up the English! I used to go down with the rest of the club and we'd enter all the events. I enjoyed the camaraderie and meeting people. I started to enter the competitions down here. That was a good reason to move down here later on in '78. I got into racing and we went to the Isle of Man for the first time in '68. In 1971 they gave me a corner, Kerr's Corner; there was also Weirs Wiggle for Ann Weir, Ronald's Elbow for John Ronald, and other

corners for Ray Kemp, Arthur Francis and a few others. I met a guy there called Nev Frost; he was the absolute dogs bollocks on a Lambretta. If you think some of the guys racing nowadays are good you should have seen him, he was exceptional.

"I moved down to England in 1978 when my Ma died; my Dad died when I was eight so my Ma was my Mother, Dad, Sister, Aunty – she did everything, she was brilliant. I was born in '46, it was after the war. When she died I thought it was time for a move for the bairns. In Scotland they've got this thing where if you're a Protestant you go to a Protestant school, if you're Catholic you go to a Catholic school. I just thought it'd be nice if they didnae have to. I got the chance to come down here through John Ronald, the Lambretta guy. He got me a job repairing artificial limbs at the City hospital in Nottingham. I was there for three years, but it was a bit of a closed shop really, a job you had for life. John's been there all his working days, God bless him. John was the prosthesis guy, making the limbs, and we worked in the background mending limbs. Another lad there was Ralph Hyde; he used to edit *Jetset* magazine.

"I fancied a change and had the gall to leave, which set the cat amongst the pigeons; most of the guys I worked with are still there! That's when I moved to selling photocopiers; I enjoyed it and made a lot of money. I was top salesman within the first three months and did very well at it, but Eric Brockway asked me to go and work at Douglas, so I left, and took a huge drop in money. I was only there a year before they pulled the plug on it in 1982. I was a storeman, but by the end of it I was doing pretty much everything.

Norrie's Vespa 90SS racer, LCI, is almost as well known as he is. It's still in race trim, but hasn't been out on a track for a decade.

Part of scootering history: will it ever get a chance to race again?

Part of Norrie's memorabilia collection includes this superb Innocenti factory, Lambretta book. It's inscribed to Peter Agg, former managing director of Lambretta Concessionaires.

"When I moved down to England I met up with Dave Webster and John Ronald, and started racing properly. It's not worth just doing a few meetings a year if you want to win a championship. I wasn't a sprog by this time, age was catching up with me. I was 37 when I won the road race championship.

"These days we can't get enough bums on seats. I don't think it's a good thing to live in the past and be an ex-racer. That's why, when the BSSO asked me to be Chairman and then President I said yes. I said I'd help out but I didn't want a vote because what I want might be totally different to what any of the current riders want. Geoff Mason, the Chairman, and the rest of the committee do a great job.

"It's a shame we don't get more support from the factories though, like the Zip Cup we ran a few years ago. It was meant to be a three year deal, but Piaggio pulled the plug after two years, Malossi was 100 percent committed.

"We need to fight hard to keep scooter racing going. Recently, I've tried to get some of the old racers involved again by giving ex-racers free membership of the BSSO and inviting them to the annual dinner dance."

What does scootering mean to you? "All of our lives in scootering are interconnected, everybody knows me, everybody knows you. We're not in it for five minutes, it's about being a part of it and, although, commercially, I'm a businessman, I'm

Pages from Mrs D. Dorman's accessory book; it must be worth a fortune to the right person.

still interested in scooters, still interested in the Vespa Club and what goes on, and I still collect all the memorabilia. I've got magazines back to 1955,

I think. I'm going to sell a load of them, though, give other people a chance to see them. I've got Japanese magazines that you read from the back to the front, and Piaggio brochures that are fantastically interesting. Eric Brockway gave me a whole load of calendars, years ago, and I eventually sold them to a guy in America.

"There's one very unusual thing I've got. Douglas didn't want to produce its own Vespa accessories, so it dealt with a French company and it sent us a book of drawings of the accessories. It also had drawings of stickers featuring Mickey Mouse and Minnie in a swimming costume to stick on scooters. It's hand-made, with a hard cover, and all these great prints. It's like rocking horse shit, nobody's ever seen one, I've never seen another one, and I've been in and out of dealers all my life. It's called 'Mrs D. Dormans, Douglas sales and service accessory booklet'. You flick through it and it's full of all these fantastic things for Vespas. You think we get some good stuff these days; we don't get anything like these. They didn't have to produce them in China either then."

Do you miss being in the shop? "I miss not knowing who your next customer would be; they'd walk in off the street or phone up and come in. You remember Howlett? Jeremy Howlett? With Dazzle? That was a smashing bike, and we did a lot of work on it. Jeremy had a lot of ideas, and it was a superb scooter when it was finished.

"It was exciting working in the shop. Every day was different, there was always something new happening, and I'm glad I did it. I enjoyed working with Dave but, by the end it got a bit tiresome. It was nothing to do with me or Dave, and I'm sure he'd say the same, but we'd both just had enough of each other, I think. I know some people have tried to print things about us but, in real terms, I just grew tired.

"The Vespa Club was doing a thing on the PX and it asked if I'd got any history. I said "Yes, I launched it, in *Scooter and Scooterist*" before it'd been launched at the Motorcycle Show!

"Eric Brockway was a great family friend; he's known my kids since they were small. He used to

Norrie's racer sits alongside another gorgeous 90SS from his collection.

come to all our open days at MSC, then, when my son, Robert went on his own for a while with Scootz, he used to come to his shop open days as well, he was a lovely man. On one occasion I jokingly referred to him as 'Dad', and I was a bit embarrassed because he showed no response when I said it, so I thought I'd put my foot in it. Then about two years later his book from Haynes came out. I'd always jibed about him never having ridden a scooter. Anyway, he came up to see me and he said, "I've got a copy of the book for you, and I've put a little inscription inside for you." He passed me the book and said he'd put a picture of me in it, so I flicked through the pages and there I was being presented with an award by the Philips electrical people. They used to give you a radio or a shaver or something. Then he flipped the page and there was a picture of him riding a scooter and he said, "See your Dad does ride scooters!" I was quite embarrassed and felt like I'd been kicked in the balls. He was a true gentleman and a hugely funny man.

"There was another time when those whistling keyrings came out. I've got it on video, and even now I wet myself laughing at it. Eric wanted to impress Ernie Hendy, a chief technician at Douglas. He used to go to the Isle of Man and repair bikes for the riders, so he was a top man. Eric had this keyring and threw it into the grass; he was eating an apple at the time and couldn't whistle properly. You had to hit a certain monotone note for the keyring to work. Ernie kept saying in his West Country accent,

"I told you it wouldn't work Eric and now you've lost your blasted keys." Eric kept walking around the long grass trying to whistle so he could find his keys. Eventually, he hit the right note and the keyring bleeped back at him. He said to Ernie, "See I told you it would work!" It went on for about ten minutes. Think about it, Eric and Ernie. It was like watching Morecambe and Wise."

What do you think to the current focus on being eco-friendly? "Green issues, that's just another tax con. 'Oh, your carbon footprint.' I'd like to stick my carbon footprint right up the European Union's jacksy!"

Many Scots like a drink, how about you? "I enjoy a beer or two, but I can't have too many, I just find I can't take too much. Once I've had two pints I'm happy, but at three I've usually had too many. I've never smoked or taken drugs either. I was taught a trick by my brother when I was little. There was a generation between us. When I was four, him and my cousin thought it'd be funny if I had to have a puff of a cigarette to get each carriage of my train set back. They made me puff on it till I went green and puked. I never touched another cigarette in my life, lit, unlit, in a packet, I won't pick them up."

Steve Foster

Anybody who has been on a national rally during the last 25 years will have bumped into Steve Foster at one time or another. Steve was the chairman of the Calverton Hornets during the club's heyday in the 1980s and early '90s. The outspoken figure is better known these days as the front man for VFM, Value for Money

Steve Foster on his regular rally scooter.

Promotions, which is, arguably, the biggest and most successful scooter rally promoter in recent times. Steve can usually be seen riding to rallies on his pearl white, Lambretta TS1, with his club-mates from the Mansfield Monsters. Although, being a rally organiser means he has to get all the PA equipment to the town, not to mention all the disco gear, records, CDs, first aid equipment, fire extinguishers, and other essential equipment needed to run a safe and successful scooter rally campsite. Usually he cajoles a volunteer to drive the VFM truck and trailer but, occasionally, he gets lumbered and the scooter has to stay at home. When Steve isn't promoting events, he usually spends his weekends at rallies and dos put on by other Scooterists. Here's what he had to say about his time in scootering.

How did you get into scootering? "I started in scootering in Calverton, a little mining village, after watching a big gang of lads riding around on old Lambrettas in the mid-seventies. I just sat and looked at them and thought, 'That's what I want

Young Mod, Steve Foster (second left) in 1981, hopes the barman will serve him but it's not looking likely!

to do'. Then, as they slowly disappeared, all the young lads, my age, started buying the scooters off them, for twenty or thirty quid and started taking them down the lanes to ride them. Then all the kind of Mod thing kicked in with *Quadrophenia* and everything, so I got myself a GP, which I paid £30 for, and got it on the road. Bought myself a parka and off I went.

"That was my gentle indoctrination into the world of scooters, really, through my peers. Lads

there. It just grew. By 1984 we'd got members from all over Nottingham and it was the foundation for what became a very tight club, more of a family than a club. It lasted like that for over a decade. 1984 was our first official year where we did every national rally in the UK, with a back-up van, all organised, which was pretty good for a load of young lads on the dole, or on low income. Then we did every rally

Steve (centre) with Nottingham's most prolific 1980s scooter club, the Calverton Hornets.

Who cares about a bit of rain when you're camping?

a lot older than me, who were Mods/ Scooter Boys with big flared trousers and parkas. They all used to go down to Skegness and always met in Calverton. There's a few of them left. We all used to kind of follow them around, hoping that they would talk to us.

"I was a Mod for a few years, and travelled the world in the army, took my scooter with me. Slowly, like so many people, I became a Scooter Boy and started wearing practical clothing for riding. Then, I just kind of drifted, musically and image-wise, into a harder image, part and parcel of the rallies really."

How did the Calverton Hornets come about? "The Hornets started through lots of lads in Calverton who were younger than me, and a lad called Graham, getting scooters. We had a club called 'The Outsiders'. It was a Mod club, and had a very select group of people from Nottingham, including ourselves. It was all a bit 'up your own arse', kind of a snobby club, and we really couldn't be doing with it any more, because we were doing more and more proper national rallies. The Calverton contingent formed the Hornets in 1983, in a pub in Calverton. We had some stickers made, held a disco to raise some money. Then we sat down and made some rules up, which we then ripped up and it went from

through the eighties and into the nineties. Our club was represented with a big turnout for a decade or so until we split up and fell out with each other. The Hornets carried on but in a slightly different vein."

How did you get into promoting? "Promotion was just a natural thing really. Running a scooter club for so long and trying to raise money without taxing your members makes you become quite imaginative. We didn't want to start charging subs and ridiculous things like that, where everybody starts falling out, so we ended up putting loads of discos on and bought our own equipment.

"The club events got that big, we were attracting over a thousand people. We also put custom shows on and other large scale events in Nottingham, and raised a lot of money at it. We did that for years and I thought 'I could make a living at this' so I started putting bands on in Nottingham."

"We'd always supported VFM and kind of worked within it, with Lowey and Nick Jolly and all the others, but it started to fall apart because a lot of

VFM founder Lowey rides pillion, and even dresses appropriately!

Nick Jolly was the other half of the partnership before Steve and Johnny took over.

them went off raving. Lowey went into the dance scene and VFM sort of collapsed. Me and Johnny Bolland thought alternative dos on rallies were important, so we carried it on. We picked up the VFM banner and took it into the early nineties. So that's how we got into putting events on at rallies, collectively, with whoever we had with us at the time. It was a natural thing, though, from putting on club events to doing VFM, just a straight forward crossover. Our club had survived by putting events on, had paid for club back-up vans and everything. Nobody ever paid membership or subs. It was just an expansion of that really, up to the present day."

Was the VFM takeover a gentleman's agreement? "Not as such, VFM has always belonged to scootering, and people saw it as some alternative fringe thing on rallies. Lowey and Nick ran it until the 1980s demise saw a lot of people leave scootering, including a lot of VFM DJs and Lowey, even Nick Jolly had had enough of rallies by then, with all the politics and trouble, so suddenly there was no VFM. All the guys who were left; myself, Johnny Bolland, and a few others who'd been involved with VFM sat around for a couple of years twiddling our thumbs, going to official dos and being a bit bored. We were getting plenty of grief from people who had been regular VFM goers, so we did the North West rally in Morecambe as an alternative event, and we just called it New VFM. We did a couple more like that, and then, eventually, we just did more and more.

"Lowey didn't mind, he knew all about it. He insisted we gave him £250 a couple of years ago, when he did a charity walk along the Great Wall of China. That was his payment for using VFM's name, although he probably doesn't know it! VFM belongs to rallies, so the same would happen if I went, or Johnny. You don't take it with you; whoever is around carries it on."

It's kind of ironic in a way because VFM has become the mainstream these days. "It's very ironic, but scootering was in the doldrums, rallies may not have continued, or certainly not continued with a national calendar, and there wouldn't have been this big resurgence. It was only through a lot of people's hard work through the mid-1990s that we're here today.

"In a way it was a moral responsibility for whoever was left organising events in the UK, to take on board what was left of the NSRA and pick up what events were worth keeping. It wasn't just VFM; there were clubs like the Olympics, Monsters, and other clubs and individuals who carried on the flag under the umbrella of the BSRA. It's ironic because it meant we had a responsibility to everybody who attended our events, rather than a kind of alternative group of people who came to our dos and, if they didn't like the music, could just fuck off. Suddenly, we had to musically cater for everybody and, if they moaned about the music, we had to do something about it, rather than say, "There's the door, go to the main do". Suddenly, we *were* the main do! We've learnt a lot from it over the years, and I think we've still managed to keep our image as alternative, off centre – where the best music is heard. Whatever we play is slightly progressive, rather than just playing the same old tunes week in week out, year in year out."

How do you think the music has changed? "VFM, to begin with, was a place where you didn't hear any soul. Lowey had four soul records, and one of those was scratched! It was an alternative disco, alternative in the sense that you may not have heard the most avant-garde punk or best kind of tunes around at the time, and you were just as likely to hear some Erasure as you were a top Smiths track or the Clash, or Stranglers. You would more than likely hear some poncy disco tune or stupid party tune. It was just an alternative party run by Scooterists. I mean, originally, VFM was set up not just because of the music but because Lowey and Nick weren't happy with outsiders running all the dos on rallies, like the All-nighter Club. Soulies running dos on rallies, these guys didn't even own scooters. Musically, it's a world away from what we play now. We use proper equipment these days, not just anything we could get our hands on. We use big PAs and professional gear.

"The music on rallies has changed, it's very subtle, but if you listen to music now and then listen to a tape from 1986 it's very different, but you always get these little trips down memory lane where the music comes back in vogue. There's a strong kind of throw back to the 1950s Psychobilly at the moment, rock & roll in mainstream music. All the young indie kids are starting to grow quiffs and get turn ups on their jeans, so that's becoming more apparent on rallies again."

What do you think to the modern scene, compared to when you started? "Now, this minute, this year, I think we're entering into a different age, we're on the cusp of something that is age related, certain traditional kind of scootering values and what people know as being traditional rallies are going to change. There's a lot of people coming into scootering now, people coming from the fifties generation of scootering. A lot of older people, we've had a born again faze, now we're getting a load of really old dodderers coming in who never knew scooter rallies in the 1980s, they never grew up with the traditional eighties rallies and don't understand why we do a rally in Morecambe Bay or somewhere. They'd rather be at some country house, parking their arses on the lawns, polishing chrome and pouring tea out of a flask! I think we're entering an age where events like that might become more

prevalent and the 3-4am bars, and all-night partying might become a thing of the past.

"In the eighties it was all new, you were on a learning curve, so you can't really compare the two. Now it's not an adventure to me, it's something that I love doing and I love seeing my friends and the community that I've grown up with, but I don't get that turning of the stomach, that quickening, the buzz. Although, when I ride to rallies I still get it.

"In the eighties you'd be turning up at somewhere like Exmouth or Brighton for the very first time and it was all unknown then. Now we've been doing it that long you know exactly what's going to happen.

"There's a lot of reminiscing at the moment, people demand this escapism to what they had twenty years ago, I don't really go for that. I prefer to move on and move forward, I'd hate to see scootering stagnate and turn into some kind of retro trip down memory lane; 'I remember when I used to get the old scooter out when I was twenty'. That's not for me and I think when it gets to that stage a lot of people, like me, might disappear."

What do you think will happen to the scene in the future? "Who knows the future, what would you have thought about the future ten years ago? I always have this memory of sitting in a house in Ramsgate when I was 18, on the run from the army, with my Lambretta. Living with this 26 year old Suedehead called Martin. He'd lived through the seventies era of scootering, I looked at him and wondered how a bloke so old could still be in to scooters. I had no vision of me in the future, being 44, riding around on my Lambretta, doing rallies, and I still haven't got that vision of doing it in another four years' time, but I probably will be. Scootering will go on, it'll adapt and change. Love it or hate it, it's the kind of thing that will perpetuate, as long as people can still get out on their Zimmer frames, take the tablets, and have a few beers! It will change because people are getting older, and we're getting into a phase now where we're predominantly forty-something. People around us are dropping dead, and we may see numbers dropping dramatically in the next few years. People get older and can't ride anymore."

Do you think the scene will become more regionalised? "I don't think the rallies are as regionalised as people say. The national events still attract people from all around the UK and abroad.

Some are regional, but they're meant to be. Locally, around the country, there's an upsurge in interest, so when there is a national on there are still plenty of people on scooters in local areas as well, because there are just more people into scooters. There will still always be events where people travel, like Bridlington and Mersea, for instance, which attract people from the north and south. People like to see each other. I think as people get into the next decade, which for many is their fifties, we'll see a whole different style of rally. What we see now at the Isle of Wight with scooters on trailers and on the back of campers will become more dominant and accepted. People won't question or moan about it as much. Rallies will probably end up with a little concourse show and a ride out. The way scootering has evolved over the last two decades will change, and we'll go back to a more genteel type of rally. It'll be a combination of a national rally and the kind of classic motorcycle rally where most of the bikes arrive on a trailer.

"There may also be a division between classic scooters and modern autos. There are loads of people getting in to the classic side of things again, and it's only a matter of time before somebody forms a classic scooter club and promotes classic scooter events, but on a larger scale; puts some big money into it. Not like the vintage Vespa club or something, but one which will encompass Vespa and Lambretta and cause a big split. Eventually, as more and more modern autos become accepted or embraced as scooters by the magazines and scooter organisations you'll get a backlash – but we'll wait and see. How far can you water this scene down? Maybe mechanised wheelbarrows will be accepted!"

Dave Porter

Dave is the Laurence Llewellyn-Bowen of scootering. He's well-known on the scooter scene as a DJ, and also runs his own internet radio show, www.scooteristradio.com.

There's no disputing the fact that Dave is different. With his bleached blonde bouffant hair do, frilly shirts, and his usual DJ'ing attire of knee length suede or leather boots it's hard not to be intrigued by him. Dave has 'Mod' running through him like the lettering in a stick of Blackpool rock, and growing up as 'the only mod in the village' was pretty hard; here's what he had to say ...

How was life for you as you grew up as a Mod in Colchester? "The early years were tough, running the gauntlet every day at school. Wearing a parka in Colchester was almost a death sentence, but once all the nob-heads had disappeared, or became 'plastic' Mods themselves it was a good place to be."

What does being a Mod mean to you personally? "Standing out from the crowd and being proud of it."

Do you think the current scene is better or worse than it's ever been? "Better, yes much better than it was. Let's face it, we are all getting older, and sometimes wiser, and the scene is still strong, so we all must be doing something right. From the 7000 plus that turn up at the Isle of Wight, to the smaller club dos, everyone who promotes on the

Dave Porter at work.

scene should pat themselves on the back for making the scene what it is today."

What would you like to see happening to improve the current scene? "Everything that could be done is being done; it's a bloody good scene."

Do you own any scooters, if so what? "Yes, at the moment a Pink PX200E Vespa named Preaching to the Perverted."

How would you describe your style of dress? "Mid- to late-sixties Kinks look, almost a Goth feel to it. A way of dress a lot of Scooterists don't like or can't handle. I think anything straying from the normal gets people on edge."

How long have you been Dj'ing and what's the highlight of your career to date? "I've been Dj'ing since I was at school, about 1978 was my first turn on the decks at the school youth club. Highlight of my whole time on the scene, at a guess would be promoting Mods May Day '99; watching 2000 Mods and ex-Mods going mental to Ian Page performing *Time For Action*. In fact, you could say any gig I do where the dance floor is packed is another highlight."

What is your best scootering memory? "Great Yarmouth, 1982. After chucking out time everyone headed back to the car park and school field camping area. After an hour the chants of 'We are the Mods' came from the car park and the whole camp site started chanting as well. The voices of 2000 plus Mod scooter riders could be heard for over an hour, with many of us making our way to the beach."

If you could choose one rally destination where would it be and why? "I would have to say the French Beetsugar rally in Amiens, always a good atmosphere, and it takes scooter rallies back to basics, how they were back in the early days. Plus a good crowd of Brits make the trip every year. Scooter clubs, such as Cucumbers SC, BDSM SC and the SBW crew just make it a great time."

How's the radio show going and what inspired

Dave entertains the crowd in his own imitable style.

you to start it? "www.scooteristradio.com has gone from strength to strength since its inception in 2006, with over 2000 Scooterists tuning in every week. It came about whilst at the IOW, with the local radio station doing a road show especially for the Scooterists and making a bad job of it. I remembered whilst working at the Essex Uni, I did a part time session on the University's Radio Station, so I decided to give it a go myself."

Would you like it to become more mainstream, what's the future for it? "I would like to take the station to mainstream radio, as in SIR on one of the digital channels on freeview, but like everything it's money."

If you could describe the scooter scene in one sentence what would it be? "A way of life you can lose yourself in, with good music and bloody good mates."

If you could be remembered for one thing what would it be? "Entertaining people."

Is there anything you'd like to add? "That old saying of behind every good man is a good woman. In my case, without the love and support from Scootergoth, AKA Mistress Fi Fi, AKA Fiona, I don't think I would have done half of the things I have in the last six years. To all my mates just keep on keeping on."

Whoever you are on the scooter scene, be it a regular rally goer who gets to every event possible, or a scooter club DJ who plays to a regular crowd. Perhaps you're just an ordinary Scooterist who spends the whole night on the dance floor, making other people watch and share in your enjoyment of the music. You could just be well known locally as a person into scooters, or a familiar sight around town. As long as you're living the life, riding your scooter and putting a positive spin on this fantastic scene, you are one of the faces.

10
Welcome to the future

The classic geared Vespa or Lambretta is still the preferred scooter of choice for the majority of road-going Scooterists. There have also been various oddments throughout the years, particularly from German manufacturers, and even the classic British marques, Triumph and BSA, but none has caught on with rally-going Scooterists like the stylish Italian two-stroke machines.

Things started to change in the late 1990s, though, as one particular manufacturer developed a scooter which would eventually kick-start a whole new generation of riders, and tempt many lifelong Scooterists away from their beloved Vespas and Lambrettas.

In 1997, Gilera, an Italian firm with a proven race heritage (now owned by Vespa producer, Piaggio), brought out a revolutionary automatic sports scooter, the Gilera Runner. Traditional scooter riders had always turned their noses up at anything slightly different to their favoured geared scooters, but word soon started to spread about the performance of this new plastic fantastic!

The original Gilera Runners were available as a two-stroke 50cc, 125cc and 180cc, and its performance was breathtaking compared to an ordinary geared scooter. The automatic transmission means the engines power is harnessed perfectly, enabling the scooter to keep up with and often beat larger capacity tuned machines.

German machines like this Zundapp Bella never really made an impact on the scene.

The fire red Gilera Runner 180 soon caught on with all kinds of rider.

The Gilera Runner was quickly adopted by youngsters and Scooterists alike. Custom paintwork and engine tuning followed soon after.

this new breed of sports scooter. Although its speedo was very optimistic, the performance was certainly a match for many tuned scooters, and it gradually started to catch on and appear on rallies, often meeting with disapproval from people who would soon be riding autos themselves!

Before the Gilera Runner was launched automatic scooters were few and far between. Machines like the Honda Melody were about as good as it got, and were hardly likely to tempt a teenager onto two wheels, never mind get a Scooterist to trade in his Vespa for one! Prior to the Runner, Piaggio had released the Hexagon and a few of these unconventional-looking scooters were seen at rallies in the 1990s, but were never taken seriously, even though they were powered by the same engine that would later be used in the Runner.

Without a doubt the Runner paved the way for a new UK scooter boom, and before long dozens of manufacturers were trying to get a piece of the new automatic scooter market.

As usual, though, the Italians, with their sense of style, and passion for creating gorgeous machines (whether on two or four wheels), were well ahead of the field. The Runner may have been the first true automatic sports scooter, but another Italian company was soon going to bring out a machine which would achieve a cult following all of its own.

The Italjet Dragster quickly developed cult status; quirky good looks and the superb Piaggio engine meant it was accepted by traditional Scooter riders; well, most of them, anyway!

People were soon claiming to have seen over 90mph on the clock of the fantastic 180cc version, and boasted about bike beating acceleration away from the lights. The Runner caught out many unwary bikers in the early days who dismissed it as 'just a moped'.

After a slow start, many Scooterists warmed to

Italjet had a long history of building small capacity bikes, especially trials bikes and mini bikes for kids, but it quickly latched on to this new auto craze. Italjet bought in the tuneable Piaggio engines (as fitted to the Runner) and developed a scooter which would become a legend. The Italjet Dragster was born.

The Italjet could only have been designed by an Italian company, and its styling, flair, and quirky good looks made it an instant hit. The Dragster had a purple steel trellis frame, quite similar to that of a Ducati, and it provided the backbone for the all important engine. Aggressive-looking, minimalist styling, a Vega style front fairing, and a bike-style rear seat unit gave the Dragster the look of a cutdown Lambretta group six race bike. The Italjet sported revolutionary hub centre steering, previously only seen on exotic Bimotas. Dropped handlebars and a chrome dash completed the styling of this modern day classic. It may not have had the smooth crisp lines of a Lambretta Grand Prix, or the bulbous shape of a Vespa, but the Italjet Dragster still turned as many heads amongst fellow scooter riders and the general public alike.

The Dragster wasn't without its problems, though. The steering didn't work as well as it looked like it should, for example, which made cornering something of a hit and miss affair. It was quite easy to get around a fast corner, but some tight bends were a case of 'Tip it in and pray you'd get round!' The heavy steel steering arm jutting out of the bottom of the front fairing made it hard for wheelie merchants to get the front end in the air, although it benefited riders once they started tuning the machines because it helped to keep the scooter under control. The Runners were much lighter, perfect for pulling wheelies.

Other problems included the rear pillion seat, which would self eject at every opportunity (driving the price of decent secondhand ones through the roof), the Paioli shock absorbers didn't last too long either, and the plastics were a bit flimsy and prone to lugs snapping off, Scooterists like things to go wrong occasionally, though, and if you don't get the tools out at least once on a journey it's a waste of time going!

The shape and style of the Dragster gave itself to customising, and it wasn't too long before the familiar fluorescent orange scooters were being re-sprayed, with race replicas becoming quite popular. The Monster Mob Ducati race team even used custom-painted Dragsters as paddock bikes for a couple of seasons.

Italian tuning giant, Malossi, had cottoned on to this new phenomenon, and quickly brought out a performance kit for the superb Piaggio 125/180 engine. The 172cc cylinder kit boosted performance and opened up a whole new world for scooter riders, and the kit would become an almost obligatory bolt on for the discerning auto owner. The Piaggio engine was a great block for tuners to work on, and some of the top scooter tuners have achieved over 36bhp after tuning the engines, even more with nitrous oxide! Other tuning goodies were soon to follow; new variators were released to improve the gearing, different roller weights to improve acceleration or top end, depending on the rider's requirements, and, of course, no two-stroke would be complete without a decent expansion pipe to harness all this extra power. For out and out horsepower, a PM59 from PM Tuning became the favourite aftermarket exhaust, but the stainless steel Scorpion system was a close second. The Scorpion didn't produce as much power as a PM, but it sounded much nicer than the ugly,

These days you're lucky to see a Dragster with a rear pillion seat in place, most were replaced by a seat pod after the original item ejected itself!

The Dragster engine, complete with tuned Malossi 172cc kit, big carb, and PM exhaust. This PSN, Ryan Saxelby-tuned scoot puts out 37bhp, and will do 115mph on the dyno.

heavy, standard system (nicknamed 'the turd'), and the stainless steel construction meant that the owner didn't have to bother re-painting it with heat resistant paint on a regular basis.

Sadly, Italjet as a company got into difficulties in 2003 and was forced to close, ending a forty-four year chapter in the history of classic bikes and scooters. Its forward-thinking designs were only with us briefly, and, although the receiver sold the remainder of its product line to Indian firm, Kinetic, we're unlikely to see them over here. Massimo Tartarini, son of the original owner of Italjet, retained the company name and rights to the Dragster and has shown prototypes of Italjet Dragsters (fitted with the latest generation four-stroke Piaggio engines). The machines still haven't made it into production at the time of writing, and it looks doubtful that we'll ever see the progression of the Dragster in our scooter shops ...

As a result of the relatively short production run and Italjet's untimely demise, spares for Dragsters have become sought after and pricey, a small, square, plastic radiator cover, for instance, can easily make £35 on eBay. Other items, like rear seat blanking plates and pillion pads, are also worth a fortune; they'll be like gold dust in another five years, so hang on to them, and they may provide a decent pension! Hindsight is a wonderful thing and I wish I'd held on to my first ever GP200, which I naively swapped for a pair of shelf-mount 25-watt speakers for my Morris Marina when I was seventeen ...

Although it took a while for autos to become accepted, or tolerated on the national rally scene, many Scooterists secretly knew that these modern, faster scooters were a much easier machine to use for long distance rally work. A 180cc, or 172cc Dragster or Runner would keep up with tuned Lambretta TS1s without too much hassle, and over a long run they'd save a fortune in petrol and two-stroke oil as well, especially when compared to gas guzzling Lambrettas. They're also more reliable. Slowly but surely the number of autos on rallies started to increase, and soon became an accepted part of the scene.

The riders of these newfangled autos were often well established rally-going Scooterists in their own right, rather than newcomers to the scene, and over the years they had religiously used Vespas and Lambrettas, often battling against all the odds to make it to a rally without getting his or her hands dirty. As a result, auto riding Scooterists were often accused of 'Going over to the dark side' and, before too long, the name stuck and 'The Darkside' became a new chapter in the history of scootering.

The Darkside isn't a club as such; it doesn't hold regular meetings or require subs to be paid each week, but members do pay to join and receive a t-shirt, stickers, and a membership card which entitles them to a 'Darkside' discount at participating scooter shops and businesses. The informal movement has grown steadily since 2004, and at present it numbers around 350 members, with an average age of 40. The Darkside even holds its own annual Euro rally which, for the past two years has been in Belgium, and it looks like the Darkside will continue to gain momentum as more and more Scooterists take to life without gears. The Darkside can be found lurking on the forum of www.scooter-scene.co.uk – may the force be with you.

If the Darkside ever needed a leader, then Exeter-based Terry Walters (AKA Tezza) is its Darth Vader.

The Darkside represents the progressive face of scootering.

SCOOTER LIFESTYLE

Here's his interpretation of the movement:

"The Darkside is all about progressive scootering. It was formed back in 2004 by a small group of Scooterists who had been attending UK and European scooter rallies for over 20 years, and had progressed on to riding modern Italian performance automatic scooters, such as the Dragster and the Runner. So we formed an association for like-minded Scooterists. Within three years the Darkside had grown to over 350 members and has since held two successful Euro rallies in Belgium. As much as the Darkside is about modern scooters it's more about the people that ride them."

The modern rally workhorse, Vespa GTS 250. Almost 80mph, hassle-free, and comfortable.

Although most of the popular scooters have been predominantly powered by revvy two-stroke engines with four gears, ever increasing Euro legislation has slowly but surely been hammering nails into their coffins. When the latest stringent Euro 3 legislation comes into effect in 2008, the humble two-stroke will be close to extinction, or, more precisely, you won't be able to buy a new one over 50cc – so hang on to your old ones and look after them. It's a sad time for us two-stroke junkies and, currently, the only geared two-stroke scooter you can buy new is the Vespa PX125, but even that machine is living on borrowed time and is set to die an untimely death once current stocks are exhausted (like the workhorse PX200 which was phased out in 2006). Manufacturers have the know-how to build cleaner burning two-stroke engines, they can even be made to produce less harmful emissions than four-strokes, but, sadly, for one reason or another they aren't prepared to do it,

The Gilera Nexus hasn't really caught on with rally-going Scooterists, but a few Darksiders have started to adopt them.

and the future will be dominated by fuel-injected, automatic, four-stroke scooters; they're reliable, and cheap to run, but ever so slightly boring to ride.

In 2004 Piaggio launched a new automatic scooter which would catch on with traditional scooter riders in a big way. The Vespa GT proudly carries on the famous name, and brings it bang up to date. Originally available as a 125cc and 200cc, this machine had the styling and all important metal monocoque frame of a Vespa, as well as its retro-styled chrome scroll badge on the legshields. The GT has a modern four-stroke automatic engine and powerful disc brakes, both front and rear, much better than the antiquated drum brakes found on most older Vespas. A top speed of almost 80mph for the 200cc version coupled with a fine handling chassis and a style not too dissimilar to the Vespa PX range (if you squint a bit) meant that many Scooterists who'd been in the closet with regards to auto scooters could suddenly 'come out' and proudly ride this modern machine, without feeling the shame of riding a 'plastic' scooter. It quickly became a winner for Piaggio, both amongst ordinary riders who wanted a dependable machine with a bit of character to commute on, and as a modern day machine readily accepted amongst most Scooterists.

The auto scooter revolution has slowly but surely caught on, and most scooter clubs boast at least a few auto riding members. Often, Scooterists will still have their beloved Lambretta or Vespa in the shed, but the auto gets used much more frequently, especially for longer trips, basically because it's just so easy to ride. You can simply load a modern automatic scooter up on the morning of a rally and thrash it until you get there without even getting your hands dirty, give it a wash afterwards and that's the extent of your maintenance done! You don't suffer from regular heat seizures, as you do on many air cooled scooters – especially tuned ones – and the power is on tap whenever you need it, so overtaking lorries on the motorway isn't a seat of the pants affair like it is with a geared scooter, which can often leave a tailback of irate motorists as you slowly creep by at virtually the same speed as the wagon, fingers carefully resting over the clutch lever waiting for the inevitable and badly timed seizure to occur. You'll be hoping and praying that you make it past the lorry and into safety before it happens! You can spot time-served traditional scooter riders on autos by looking at the fingers on the left hand, they involuntarily rest over the non-existent clutch lever waiting for the scooter to 'nip up' like their old Lambretta used to do. Twenty years of riding in this way is a hard habit to shake off, and Scooterists of pension age will suffer with clutch lever induced arthritis in the future!

The popular Vespa GT range has since been superseded by the GTS. Launched in 2005 the GTS 250

The GTS 250 is a very useable rally machine; you hardly even need a toolkit!

The limited edition Vespa GTV60 is a slight variation on the GTS theme. It gives a modern twist to the early Vespa models.

quickly became a classic and readily-accepted scooter, largely due to it's larger capacity, fuel-injected engine. It's possible to see 90mph on the clock, though this is rather optimistic, a more realistic figure being 80mph. A few retro touches on the GTS include a fold out chrome rear carrier (ideal for bungeeing bags onto for rally use) and polished, flip-out pillion pegs. The GTS also has a neat digital screen which gives trip distance, fuel level, temperature and time – all 'mod' cons for the modern Scooterist! The GTS 250 can be seen at any scooter event in the UK, and it's also developed quite a large following in America and Europe, making it a true classic machine. The very latest variation on the theme is the limited edition Vespa GTV 60, a retro-styled GTS variant complete with naked chrome handlebars and a mudguard-mounted headlight, just like the very first Vespa which rolled off the production line in 1946.

Scooter manufacturers never keep still for too long and Piaggio and Gilera have both recently launched the latest crop of modern automatic scooters. Piaggio was the first to launch the fantastic MP3, a scooter but not as we know it! The Piaggio MP3 has the back end of the Piaggio X8, but the front has been treated to a strange-looking parallelogram suspension unit and twin front wheels. The concept was originally thought up by Italjet and badged as the Scoop, but the company's

The MP3 offers superior handling and stability to an ordinary two-wheeler, superb in the wet or dry!

The Gilera GP800 – 850cc, V-twin engine, 75hp. (Courtesy Mau Spencer)

demise meant it never saw the light of day and Piaggio cleverly bought the idea. The result is a scooter which can lean and out-handle virtually any two-wheeled bike or scooter on the road. The MP3 is available in both 125cc and 250cc form, using the tried-and-tested QUASAR engine as fitted to the GTS. There's also a 400cc version using the potent MASTER engine, as fitted to the X8 400.

Perhaps the MP3 is a bit too conformist-looking for most Scooterists, but anybody who has ridden one has been converted to this astounding but relatively simple technology, and there's a seriously mean-looking alternative available if you want one ...

Piaggio's sister company, Gilera has taken on the three-wheeled concept and created a monster. The Gilera Fuoco 500 uses the same technology as the MP3, but it's fitted the 492cc twin-spark MASTER engine and given the styling a massive overhaul to build a fearsome-looking scooter; pure Armageddon style, and a fantastic machine to ride. With Scooter Boys in mind Gilera has even painted it matt black, which saves the

The Gilera Fuoco takes the concept a stage further, and even comes in the Scooter Boys' favourite matt black. (Courtesy Phil Masters)

'Scooter scum' type of owner the trouble of spraying it in their preferred colour when they get the beast home!

The modern crop of super-scooters includes tourers, sports scooters, and commuters, with engines ranging in size from 400cc to the latest 850cc Gilera GP800, a 75 horsepower twin-cylinder machine capable of 114mph. The big scooters may not have had much of an impact on rally-going Scooterists just yet, but it's only a matter of time before the average age and disposable income starts to dictate what they ride for long distance work.

Whether you love the idea of being converted to an auto or not they're here to stay and will only become more popular as time goes on. They may not sound as gorgeous as a Lammy with a nice expansion pipe and big carb, but they're the future and there's no need to be afraid.

The modern scooter scene has something to offer everybody, whether it's a hard partying weekend away, a leisurely Sunday ride out with a group of friends on vintage Lambrettas, a race meeting or a parts fair. You name it, and there's an event on to suit your needs; usually not too far from home.

These days the scene has become increasingly regionalised. People from Yorkshire will tend to stick to rallies in the north, whereas Southerners tend to stick to rallies like Camber Sands and the Isle of Wight . Ten years ago people travelled many more miles. Maybe it's old age creeping in, or the cost of replacing Lambrettas and vintage Vespas, which prevents owners from thrashing the life out of them as much as they used to. There are still a good number of hard core regular rally goers who will ride to and attend every event, no matter how far away from home, and there are more than enough scooter riders in every area to keep the scene buzzing for many years to come.

We're spoilt for choice with the variety of events, from holiday camp rallies to scooter-only roughing it weekends in the countryside. We also have an abundance of specialist magazines to choose from, including the three Morton's titles, *Scootering*, *Classic Scooterist Scene* and *Twist & Go*. Other independent magazines include, *Shed Magazine*, which caters for grass roots Scooterists, and *PETROL*, a modern auto mag. Depending on which side of the traditional scooter fence you sit, Vespa or Lambretta, you can also choose from the long-standing Lambretta Club of Great Britain magazine, *Jetset* or Vespa Club of Britain's, *Vespa News*. If the magazines don't give you all the news and information you need you can always log on to one of the many scooter internet sites and forums, which pop up on a daily basis. They will answer most questions and give advice on tuning and forthcoming events, or provide a spot of light-hearted banter.

There's one thing for sure, and that's scooter riding and the people, places and lifestyle that surrounds them is here to stay. It doesn't matter if you're sixteen or sixty, you'll be made welcome, providing, of course that you've got that burning passion for those little Italian machines.

Whatever the future may hold, be it legislation to try and force us off the roads on our old two-stroke scooters (as the Italians tried to implement in 2007), or futuristic H2O fuel conversions to run the next generation of highly-tuned two-stroke scooters on little more than tap water, or even faster, more exciting four-strokes, we'll be there one way or another, propping up the bar at a favourite rally destination in a town near you!

Mine's a pint; I'll see you there.

What could be better than to spend a Sunday morning out with a few hundred friends?

Scooter-only camping rallies are becoming popular at the moment, though the seaside rally is still where the heart and soul of scootering lies.

SCOOTERS
THE TOP BRANDS

SILENCERS **Sito** GENUINE SPARE PARTS

Scorpion

HUTCHINSON

ATHENA

polini

GIANNELLI SILENCERS

DELLORTO

G.P.R. by I.Q.G.I.

HTF HIGH TECH FRICTION

KUNDO

LeoVince TNT RACING
EXHAUST SYSTEMS

MALOSSI

and many more including :- GPT - Digital Parts
FACO - Chrome Accessories - DIEFFE - Custom Seats
BCD - Custom Bodywork - CEAB - Electronic CDI's & more

**Scooter - Classic/Auto
Lightweight M/Cycle
ATV - Quad**

**Exclusive UK Sole Official Importer of
many top brands supplying UK dealers
with some of the world's best brands -
at the best prices. Contact your local
VE dealer at www.ve-uk.com/postcode**

**WEBSITE
www.ve-uk.com
EMAIL
sales@ve-uk.com**

Also from Veloce Publishing –

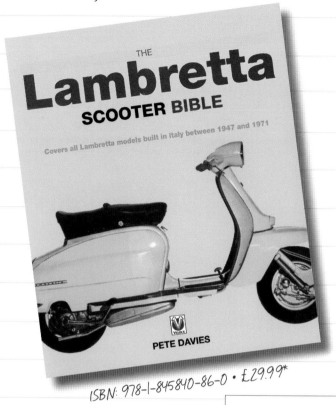

THE
Lambretta
SCOOTER BIBLE

Covers all Lambretta models built in Italy between 1947 and 1971

PETE DAVIES

ISBN: 978-1-845840-86-0 • £29.99*

The A-Z
of popular scooters & microcars

Cruising in style!

Michael Dan

ISBN: 978-1-845840-88-4 • £29.99*

Lambretta
Ll series scooters

ANDREA & DAVID SPARROW

ISBN: 978-1-904788-81-2 • £9.99*

www.veloce.co.uk

Index